THE HOME ORCHARD
HANDBOOK

QUARRY

WITHDRAWN

→ THE ←
HOME ORCHARD
HANDBOOK

A Complete Guide to Growing
Your Own Fruit Trees Anywhere

Cem Akın • Leah Rottke

BEVERLY MASSACHUSETTS

QUARRY BOOKS

First published in the United States of America by
Quarry Books, a member of
Quayside Publishing Group
100 Cummings Center
Suite 406-L
Beverly, Massachusetts 01915-6101
Telephone: (978) 282-9590
Fax: (978) 283-2742
www.quarrybooks.com

Library of Congress Cataloging-in-Publication Data is available

ISBN-13: 978-1-59253-712-9

ISBN-10: 1-59253-712-X

9 8 7 6 5 4 3 2 1

Design: Rachel Fitzgibbon, studio rkf

Chef Tal Ronnen recipes and photos are reprinted with permission from
The Conscious Cook © 2009 Tal Ronnen and Melcher Media

Printed in China

Cem

For those who sail the seas of life riding the winds of compassion for all living beings;
in particular, Ömer and Meral Akın: parents, teachers, friends.

Leah

For my students; let your care of plants and trees be your privilege, and your joy.

The Fruit Tree Planting Foundation

This handbook was made possible through the collective experience of our award-winning nonprofit charity: The Fruit Tree Planting Foundation (FTPF). With a strong belief that planting fruit trees is the most comprehensive strategy to creating healthy environments, FTPF programs alleviate world hunger, combat global warming, strengthen communities, and improve the surrounding air, soil, and water. Our orchards are strategically donated where the harvest best serves the public for generations, at places such as schools, low-income neighborhoods, city parks, community gardens, Native American reservations, international hunger relief sites, and animal sanctuaries.

FTPF collaborates with diverse communities and households across the globe, from the United States to Brazil to India to Kenya. Our programs mobilize local environmental efforts and inspire activists of all ages to get involved by putting trees in the ground. In our hunger relief programs, families are gifted with saplings and trained on how to care for the trees over time, providing a harvest year after year, rather than a food handout that can be depleted in a short time.

This book draws on FTPF's experience in the field, working under a wide range of conditions, to provide detailed instructions on how to create your own home orchard.

A portion of the proceeds from this handbook go to the Fruit Tree Planting Foundation in support of its groundbreaking mission to benefit the environment, human health, and animal welfare—all at once by planting fruit trees for communities across the world. To learn more about this important work, please visit www.ftpf.org.

CONTENTS

CHAPTER 6: Pruning and Weeding

CHAPTER 7: Prevention, Troubleshooting, and Controls

CHAPTER 8: Enjoying the Harvest

CHAPTER 9: Beyond the Home Orchard

chapter one

FRUIT TREE 101

Imagine providing essential nutrition and oxygen by the tons to humans and animals; cleansing the air, water, and soil; creating vibrant ecosystems for birds and bees; empowering individuals to become healthy stewards of their environment; and inspiring them to spread that message—addressing world hunger, global warming, and deforestation, all at once.

ONE MIGHT SPECULATE THE NEED FOR entire armies of environmentalists, health crusaders, and animal welfare activists to accomplish this. Yet, there is a singular strategy that can kick-start the heart of this process all on its own—a global catalyst for a healthy planet, if we all act together, perfectly utilizing physics, chemistry, and the symbiotic means offered by Mother Nature to nourish the world and all its inhabitants. Best of all, it is a simple, grounding, long-lasting, Earth-connecting strategy that is part of a most enjoyable journey and rewarding destination: Plant a fruit tree, care for it, encourage everyone you know to do the same, and pass on the legacy.

Simply put, trees heal the planet, from filtering air pollutants to recharging groundwater to creating healthy microcosms in the soil. And it doesn't stop there. If that tree is a fruit tree, harvest abounds for decades, sometimes centuries, improving health for generations. Excess harvests may be donated to local food banks or given to neighbors, promoting sustainability by displacing many environmental hazards associated with the mass commercial production, transportation, and packaging of most food sold in today's markets.

"The best time to plant a tree was twenty years ago. The next best time is now."

—CHINESE PROVERB

Plums ready for harvest

Fruit trees originated in the wild, ages ago.

At the table, science shows that eating more fruits cuts the risk of major diseases.[1] In the backyard, home orchards serve as a place to forge deep connections with family, friends, and nature. In the community, planting and maintaining fruit trees can be a truly holistic, tangible solution to many of the world's critical problems.

Fruit trees play an important role in the history of Earth. Many wild varieties have been around for millions of years in various forms. Fossilized remnants from the olive's ancestor date back 20 million years.[2] Early incarnations of the plant that has become the modern-day Rosaceae family, which includes apples, pears, quinces, almonds, cherries, plums, and apricots, were present 40 to 50 million years ago.[3]

And perhaps the most fruitful symbiotic relationship ever between plant and animal goes back 80 million years, when fig wasps became the exclusive pollinators of fig trees—a relationship that exists to this day.[4] Experts estimate that the earliest human domestication of fruit trees, especially olives, dates, and figs, occurred in the late Stone Age through the early Bronze Age (as early as about 9000 B.C.E. for figs).[5]

[1] Food and Agriculture Organization of the United Nations. 2001. "Human Vitamin and Mineral Requirements." Report of a joint FAO/WHO expert consultation (Bangkok, Thailand).

[2] Therios, I. 2009. *Olives*. (Biddles Ltd.: UK).

[3] Juniper, B.E. and D.J. Mabberley. 2006. *The Story of the Apple*. (Timber Press, Inc.: Portland, Ore.).

[4] Machado, C., et al. 2005 May 3. "Critical review of host specificity and its coevolutionary implications in the fig/fig-wasp mutualism." Proceedings of the National Academy of Sciences of the United States of America.

[5] Kislev, M., et al. 2006 Jun 2. "Early domesticated fig in the Jordan Valley." *Science*. 312:57–78.

Ancient Orchard Poetry

In one of the earliest recorded descriptions of a home orchard, thousands of years ago, Greek poet Homer wrote:

"Close to the gates a spacious garden lies,
From storms defended and inclement skies.
Four acres was the allotted space of ground,
Fenced with a green enclosure all around.
Tall thriving trees confess'd the fruitful mould:
The reddening apple ripens here to gold.
Here the blue fig with luscious juice o'erflows,
With deeper red the full pomegranate glows;
The branch here bends beneath the weighty pear,
And verdant olives flourish round the year,
The balmy spirit of the western gale
Eternal breathes on fruits, unthought to fail:
Each dropping pear a following pear supplies,
On apples apples, figs on figs arise:
The same mild season gives the blooms to blow,
The buds to harden, and the fruits to grow."[6]

[6] Homer. *The Odyssey of Homer* (Book VII), translated by Alexander Pope, 2010 (eBooks@Adelaide).

Home orchards have existed since ancient times, on fertile grounds such as these in the Mediterranean region.

Some trees, such as olives, can survive for more than a thousand years, making them living artifacts. Others, like apples and pears, can produce fruit for centuries. It has even been suggested that the longevity of domesticated fruit trees provides such a strong connection to the land that this bond contributed to the development of modern city-states and nations.[7] Imagine, humankind being inspired to develop sophisticated social structures based partly on a desire to be close to their beloved orchards!

Indeed, a certain indescribable magic surrounds fruit trees, as flowers metamorphose into nature's perfect foods, enchanting children and adults alike. The tree combines all the most amazing botanical processes to create a fruit so tasty that it can entice an animal to eat it and distribute the seed. What a concept!

To help share that magic and wonder, the basics of growing fruit trees in a home orchard are covered in the following chapters, including site and plant selection, planting techniques, and aftercare. These principles are applicable to nut trees as well. All

The tranquility of a sunrise above fruit trees in the tropics

[7] Janick, J. 2005. "The origin of fruits, fruit growing, and fruit breeding." *Plant Breeding Rev.* 25:255–320.

instructions promote organic, humane methods, resulting in the most sustainable Earth- and animal-friendly orchards possible that set the highest standard for others to emulate.

Imagine a place where you can have a summer picnic under the shade of a fruit tree, breathe the clean air it generates, watch the beautiful birds and other wildlife foraging in its canopy, and bring only an appetite for the healthy fruits growing overhead. Now imagine that place being in your own yard.

"To exist as a nation, to prosper as a state, and to live as a people, we must have trees."

—THEODORE ROOSEVELT

Peach blossoms waiting to be transformed into fruit.

Home orchard sustainability, with bushels of organic harvest

ENVIRONMENTAL BENEFITS

To review the research showing just how beneficial trees are for the environment and the home orchard, let's start with the air. Each year, a mature tree can produce up to 260 pounds (118 kg) of oxygen,[8] remove harmful ozone pollutants from the lower atmosphere that contribute to smog, and sequester between 35 and 800 pounds (16 and 363 kg) of carbon dioxide from the air.[9] Dwarf fruit trees are typically smaller in stature than shade trees, thus fall on the lower end of this range, while standard-size fruit trees much higher. According to scientists at the U.S. Department of Agriculture (USDA),

the planting of any type of tree is known to play a "significant role" in reducing air pollution by "… absorbing gaseous pollutants, binding soluble pollutants to their surfaces, intercepting large particulates on bark, and sequestering CO_2 in woody tissue." [10] In other words, trees act as natural air filters and oxygen tanks.

[8] This means that two medium-size trees can produce all the oxygen one person needs to breathe every year.

[9] McPherson, E.G. 2005 Apr 1. "Trees with Benefits." *American Nurseryman.*

[10] Geiger, J. G. and E. G. McPherson. 2005 Apr 27. "Trees equal clean air according to new research—Arbor Day is perfect time to plant more." Press Release. USDA Forest Service, Pacific Southwest Research Station, Center for Urban Forest Research.

Fruit trees come in small, medium, large, and extra-large varieties—all of which serve as vigilant protectors of the Earth's air, water, and soil resources. Large fruit trees, such as mangoes, can grow up to 100 feet (30.5 m) tall. Jackfruit trees can grow more than 70 feet (21.3 m) and hold the world's record for largest fruits produced— weighing in at up to 100 pounds (45.4 kg) *each*! By those standards, the jackfruit pictured here is still a baby.

Above: Standard apple trees, like this one, can reach a height of about 40 feet (12.2 m) and produce hundreds of pounds of oxygen every year, along with one of nature's most perfect meals.

Below: Dwarfing fruit trees, like this citrus, are selected to be smaller and fit into tighter spaces, yet still have significant environmental benefits.

Trees conserve valuable energy resources by naturally cooling homes in the summer and warming them in the winter. The relief of a shady tree on a hot day spent outdoors is legendary, and the same principle applies to buildings kept cool in the shade. Trees also transpire, meaning they release water through leaves, resulting in a cooling of the surrounding air. According to the director of the USDA's Center for Urban Forest Research, a difference of up to 9°F (13°C) has been observed between urban centers and their more densely forested and vegetated suburbs—along with a reduction in structural cooling costs of 25 percent from just three well-placed 25-foot (7.6-m)–tall backyard trees.[11]

Even greater savings are achieved with additional trees. In colder months, trees create effective wind blocks that prevent cold air from entering homes, a benefit that lasts throughout winter for evergreens, translating to a 10 to 12 percent savings in annual heating,[12] and as much as 50 percent according to the USDA.[13] The combined heating and cooling benefits of backyard trees result in significantly reduced energy consumption and its respective power plant output.

[11] McPherson, E.G. 2005 Apr 1. "Trees with benefits" *American Nurseryman*.

[12] Ibid.

[13] USDA Forest Service. Homeowner Resources. Available online at: www.na.fs.fed.us.

Bark functions as a living air filter to remove particulates.

In addition to lowered cooling, heating, and grocery bills (in the case of fruit trees), mature trees have been estimated to add, on average, 10 percent to a property's value.[14] A single medium-size mature fruit tree can be valued at many thousands of dollars on its own, as shown in these examples.

[14] USDA Forest Service. Homeowner Resources. Availablea online at: www.na.fs.fed.us.

Trees soak up rainfall before returning much of it to the atmosphere as vapor through transpiration and evaporation. This reduces the volume of storm runoff, notorious for washing contaminants into local bodies of water and washing away valuable topsoil. A portion of the trapped water, whether rainfall or irrigation, percolates down beyond the root system and contributes to groundwater recharge—an important element to any sustainable water management plan. Roots also anchor soil to prevent erosion from wind or precipitation, while canopies lessen the eroding impact of heavy precipitation on the ground beneath.

WELL-BEING

Ultimately, an abundant harvest is the pot of gold at the end of the rainbow for the home orchardist. Under professional, commercial settings, a fruit tree can produce hundreds of pounds of fruit each year. At home, depending on the type, age, and size of the tree, a healthy annual yield is likely to be more manageable, closer to the 40-to-70-pound (18-to-32-kg) range.

Published research is clear on the myriad of health benefits from increasing fruit consumption, including reducing incidence of heart disease, stroke, cancers, high blood pressure, low bone mineral density, and obesity, to name just a few. A United Nations panel resoundingly recommended increased fruit in the diet: "Households should select predominantly plant-based diets rich in a variety of vegetables and fruits … The evidence that such diets will prevent or delay a significant proportion of non-communicable chronic diseases is consistent."[15] The home orchard presents an opportunity for the entire family to realize healthy nutrition from having more fresh fruit available as an alternative to buying packaged, environmentally destructive, potentially illness-causing, chemically laden, nutritionally void products.

There's more. Trees radiate a profound effect on mental health and well-being. Studies from the Human–Environment Research Laboratory (University of Illinois) report that when people are around trees, mental fatigue and irritability are reduced.[16] According to Dr. Roger Ulrich of Texas A&M University, "… visual exposure to settings with trees has produced significant recovery from stress within five minutes."[17] *Five minutes.*

Research funded by the Japanese government found that exposure to forest settings lowered stress and blood pressure, and boosted immunity.[18] At the University of Florida's Institute of Food and Agriculture Sciences, researchers concluded that horticultural therapy—a therapeutic program of growing plants such as trees for those with mental or physical disorders—has been used for centuries with the following benefits: reducing physical pain, stress, and anger, enhancing productivity and problem solving, improving memory and concentration, and teaching responsibility.[19] Turns out, fruit trees are good for more than just the body—we can add mind and spirit to the equation.

The following chapters provide detailed instructions on how to realize all the benefits of a home orchard in the most Earth-friendly

[15] Food and Agriculture Organization of the United Nations. 2001. "Human Vitamin and Mineral Requirements." Report of a joint FAO/WHO expert consultation (Bangkok, Thailand).

[16] Human-Environment Research Laboratory, University of Illinois at Urbana–Champaign. *Cooler in the Shade.* Newsletter Vol. 1 No. 6.

[17] *Organic Gardening.* Nov 2007–Jan 2008 (p 61).

[18] Tsunetsugu, Y., et al. 2010. Trends in research related to "Shinrin-yoku" (taking in the forest atmosphere or forest bathing) in Japan. *Environmental Health and Preventive Medicine.* 15:27–37

Cherries ready for harvest

manner. As we have seen, planting fruit treesstands tall within the landscape of good environmental deeds, emerging as a holistic vehicle to positively impact our planet's vital signs. What better place to start than in your yard. Onward, toward a greener, more fruitful tomorrow!

[19] Worden, E.C., T. M. Frohne and J. Sullivan. 2004. Horticultural IFAS Publication #ENH970.

"Train up a fig tree in the way it should go, and when you are old sit under the shade of it."

—CHARLES DICKENS

Studies show that being around trees of any type can instantly reduce stress and enhance productivity.

Two Tigers, One Rat, and a Fig
(adapted from an ancient Zen tale)

One fine morning, in order to revive my constitution and invigorate my mind, I decided to take a walk in the forest. Absorbed in my thoughts, surrounded by the quiet wisdom of the trees surrounding me, a sense suddenly rushed over me that I was not alone.

Albeit at a safe distance, I saw a large tiger, stealthily slipping in and out of the partial cover provided by large fern leaves, moving at my exact pace and in my direction. Being a cautious man, I did not believe this to be a coincidence. I hastened my pace. Lamentably, so did the tiger, who was no longer using the foliage for cover. Little by little, my haste turned into a true sense of panic. I found myself running as fast as I could, with the tiger in strong pursuit. Suddenly, like a train coming to an emergency stop, my sprint was interrupted by a deep precipice bordering a green valley below. Almost instinctively, I grabbed a vine hanging by the side of the cliff and started climbing down.

Feeling that this heroic exertion was about to pay off, I noticed that the now familiar panting of the tiger was as loud as if I was sitting by her side. In fact, the more I descended, the louder it became. I stopped and looked down. There was another tiger panting with anticipation, below.

Clearly, the situation was less than favorable. However, I was still confident that my patience would rule the outcome and I could make an escape once one of the tigers realized that this prey was far too reluctant to comply. Just then, a new sound filled the air. This was the unmistakable gnawing cadence that only a rodent could produce. Apparently, my vine was now an incisor-filing-instrument for a field rat who no doubt heard the commotion and wanted to join in on the excitement.

Only at this moment of utter despair, I noticed a ripe fig, just within my reach, hanging from a branch on a small tree anchored to a cliff ledge. Belied by its dwarf figure, the tree had converted the fresh air, bright sunlight, and morsels of water and minerals provided by the cliff side into oversized figs oozing with aroma.

Miraculously, all sense of catastrophe lifted. I plucked the fig and placed it, skin and all, between my lips, which were spontaneously parted by a smile. I savored the sweet, crunchy delights of the fruit that had been offered by nature for that singular joyful encounter, at that particular moment, on that fine day.

chapter two

SITE SELECTION

The ideal place to plant an orchard is midway up an east-facing slope on gently rolling land, with a loam soil from 4 to 9 feet (1.2 to 2.7 m) deep. (Those of us residing in urban areas may now throw back our heads and laugh heartily.) This chapter breaks down each of the elements that make that mythic slope idyllic to illustrate how to use available space for the best advantage of fruit trees.

PLEASE NOTE THAT MOST PRODUCTIVE, healthy orchards get along someplace other than Eden. The familiar saying, "Right tree, right place," is true, and sometimes easier said than done. Taking whatever steps are needed to ensure that trees will be located where their requirements are best met *before planting* saves time and resources later, and prevents struggling with trees failing to thrive.

ROOM ENOUGH FOR FRUIT TREES

The first element of that "right place" is space: enough room for the mature canopy the tree will have someday, and enough room for tree roots to spread. Tree roots do not form a mirror image of the top growth's branch structure below ground. Instead, about 90 percent of roots live in the top 2 feet (0.6 m) of soil, especially the small roots that absorb water, nutrients, and oxygen. Roots spread outward from the tree's trunk in the upper layers of soil to distances between 1½ to 3 times the height of the tree.

Opposite page: Adjust planting distances according to your goals for the orchard site. Plant trees slightly close to create a windbreak or farther apart to create more open spaces to socialize. These trees were planted at 15-foot (4.6 m) intervals to allow easy access to all sides of the tree.

This page: Fruit trees can thrive under many different conditions, even when the ideal situation (i.e., rolling hills with good sun exposure and near water), pictured here, is not available.

So, for enough room between trees for those on standard and semidwarfing rootstocks, plant a minimum of 10 to 15 feet (3 to 4.6 m) apart. In general, the closer the planting, the more pruning will be needed to maintain adequate distance between them. Trees on true dwarfing rootstocks may be placed as close as 6 feet (1.8 m) apart. (Details about rootstocks are described in chapter 3, Plant Selection.)

Plant trees a minimum of 10 feet (3 m) from structures: buildings, patios, pools, water, sewer and gas lines, septic system leach lines—and be wary of overhead obstructions such as power lines. Always think about what trees will do underground as well as above. Spacing fruit trees properly helps to create ease of fruit harvesting and tree maintenance as well.

10–15 ft. (3–4.6 m) for semidwarfs

15 ft. (4.6 m) or more for standards

6–10 ft. (1.8–4.6 m) for dwarfs

Plant most standard fruit trees roughly 15 feet (4.6 m) apart, semidwarfing trees 10 to 15 feet (3 to 4.6 m) apart, and dwarfs a minimum of 6 feet (1.8 m) apart. Hedgerow plantings require extra maintenance and can be planted 3 feet (0.9 m) apart.

SUNLIGHT

Sunlight powers all life on Earth; this starts with plants converting the sun's energy into sugars. Fruit trees need to be planted in full sun, which means a minimum of six to eight hours of direct sunlight per day. For trees planted in hot climates, getting those direct sun hours in the first half of the day, with an afternoon break delivered by the shadows of buildings or larger trees, can be helpful.

Take a walk, and a look, around the prospective orchard site at different times of the day; watch where the sun shines and where the shadows fall. Checking this during the height of the growing season will provide a good benchmark; if practical, learn about the sun patterns on the orchard site during different seasons of the year. The sun sits lower in the sky through the winter months, stretching the length of shadows.

Morning

Afternoon

Late afternoon

This tree placement receives at least eight hours of direct sunlight a day, as shown by these photos taken throughout the day, with the last showing the desired late-afternoon shade. In the northern hemisphere, south-facing sites receive the most sun energy. When planting multiple trees, consider placing shorter varieties (e.g., dwarfs) out of the future shadow of larger ones (e.g., standards) by placing the former in front with relation to the prevailing sunlight.

AIR CIRCULATION

Go outside and get some air. Consider air circulation through the orchard site. Air that flows freely around and through trees helps prevent disease, moderates temperature, and maintains CO_2 levels for leaves. Leaves take in carbon dioxide and release oxygen during *photosynthesis*, the process of making sugars from sunlight. Good air circulation does not include a harsh, driving wind, which can cause trees to grow in unwanted directions.

Above: Strong prevailing or predictable winds from a single direction can distort the growth pattern of tree canopies.

Below: Tall hedges or other wind-breaks, such as this ivy-covered trellis, can be used to prevent directional growth when strong, prevailing winds are present.

SOIL

Soil does more than just anchor trees in place. Healthy soil can be viewed as a living organism, and will be discussed in greater detail later. One of the basic metrics for soil involves the pH scale, which measures relative acidity or alkalinity. From 1 to 14, neutral is measured at 7.0. Soils with a pH less than 7.0 are increasingly acid, greater than 7.0 increasingly alkaline. Most plants and trees thrive at a soil pH between 6.5 and 7.5. Testing the pH at a site can be as easy as obtaining a portable kit.

Additionally, during site selection, soil simply needs to be workable and drain well. *Workable* means that the soil can be dug with hand tools such as a spade relatively easily; a superhero's assistance is not required, in other words. This also means that the soil is sufficiently deep to support trees. A couple feet (0.6 m) of purchased topsoil thrown onto an abandoned concrete slab will not work. Dreamy loams, tens of feet deep, exist in many parts of the world—generally in *other* parts of the world, not your site. Three feet (0.9 m) deep is a good minimum.

A soil that is not workable does not mean the site cannot be planted; difficult soils can sometimes be corrected *before* planting. Basic information on working with soils is given in the fertilization section of chapter 5, Irrigation and Fertilization. For really difficult or damaged soils, get some assistance to find out what steps to take, before sinking a lot of time, energy, and resources into a battle with a tough soil. Regional governments, in association with universities, often provide information about local soil types. Contact the local Agricultural Extension office (called "Cooperative Extension" in the U.S.) or farm advisor to get some expert advice on a number of topics, including the best strategies to correct a soil problem.

Know Your Substrate!

The more planting you do, the more you will discover many buried treasures. FTPF has unearthed piles of rocks, old shoes, mattresses, and even an uncharted water line or two. Take a shovel to the planting site and explore the soil a bit to avoid any potential obstacles. Compacted soils or construction fill can make manual digging difficult, so always test dig a hole to ensure the orchard can be planted without the need for additional equipment. If it is possible to dig a planting hole in less than half an hour with a spade shovel and pickax, if necessary, then the planting should go smoothly.

At one particular orchard site at a school in California, the soil seemed a bit compacted, so an area was tested and found to be workable manually with a shovel, though a handheld mechanical auger was brought just in case. After about half an hour of enduring the metallic sounds of shovels bouncing off the ground without making the slightest dent, the auger was unveiled with much anticipation. As it spun into the unrelenting ground for two whole minutes, with the weight of four adult men pressing down, there was collective astonishment when the device was set aside to reveal a ping-pong ball–size hole only. This was some seriously compacted soil! Needless to say, the next call was for a tractor-mounted auger, which completed the job to perfection.

The lesson learned was, for planting trees in several places in your backyard, or even for planting larger orchards, be sure to test the workability of the soil in numerous spots as there can be great variation in even the shortest of distances.

SOIL DRAINAGE

What is soil *drainage*? Why is it necessary for good tree growth? Soil drainage is a term describing the way water moves through a soil—how quickly it soaks in, how it spreads out inside the soil as it moves through, and how long the soil stays moist between waterings. Leaves use carbon dioxide, but roots need oxygen. They respire, just like we do. Ideally, half of soil is empty space. These little empty spaces inside soil are called *pores*. A soil's pore space ought to be filled with both air and water, about 50/50. Immediately after rain or irrigation they may be filled mostly with water, and just before watering, mostly with air.

A well-draining soil is one that lets water penetrate, without pooling on the surface or running off. How fast and how much water hits the soil's surface and whether the ground is flat or sloped affects this. The soil itself and its mineral components of sand, silt, and clay, and their relative proportions, also play a big role in the *infiltration rate*.

Sandy soils accept water easily, allowing it to penetrate deeply, quickly. They also dry out rapidly, and water does not form a lateral fan pattern of moisture in the soil (making water available to more roots) but forms a straight, narrow column through, and past, the precious top 18 to 24 inches (45.7 to 61 cm) of soil, where most roots occur. Sandy soils do not hold a good reserve of moisture and are typically of low fertility.

Clay soils often have very slow infiltration rates, which can lead to puddles on the surface with dry soil underneath. Wet clay is sticky and gunky to work with. It also dries out more slowly and holds water very well—sometimes so tightly that plant roots cannot pry it loose! Most soils fall outside these two extremes and are a combination of varying proportions of sand, silt, and clay particles.

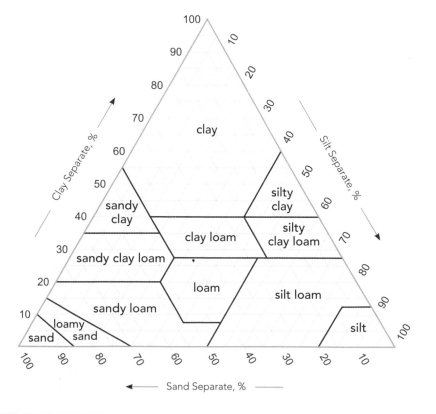

Soil consists of particles that are fine (clay), medium (silt), or coarse (sand)—or all three—in size. This soil triangle diagram illustrates the content of different soil types (courtesy of Natural Resources Conservation Service, USDA).

To find out how well the prospective planting site's soil drains, try this test:

1. Dig a planting hole for a typical containerized tree, about 18 inches (45.7 cm) deep and wide.

2. Fill the hole with water and wait while it drains out.

3. Fill the hole with water again, as soon as the first filling drains out. Now watch and note the time it takes for this second filling to drain out.

Less than five minutes? Very sandy soils drain this quickly. Between half an hour to twelve hours? Congratulations on having a well-draining soil. Still eyeing a muddy little pond at the bottom of the hole two days later? Slow-draining soils that are wet for prolonged periods cause tree roots to die for lack of oxygen. Growing trees in such conditions requires longer intervals between irrigations to allow the soil to dry out a little and let air back into the soil's pore space. Or consider choosing alternative types of planting sites such as raised beds (discussed in more detail later in this chapter).

Above Left: Soil can be tested by moistening and squeezing it in your fist. Sandy soils break apart easier than clay soils, which tend to remain in a ribbon, as illustrated here.

Above Right, Below Right: Conduct a basic drainage test prior to choosing the planting site. Dig a hole, fill with water, let drain, and fill immediately again with water. Soils with good drainage will be empty within twelve hours of the second filling.

WATER

Trees flourish along the riverbank because that's where the water is. Is the average annual rainfall that the prospective planting site receives sufficient to sustain fruit trees? Peach trees, for example, need approximately 36 inches (91.4 cm) of water per year, with the majority of that available during the last sixty days of fruit ripening. Overall, most types of fruit trees need between 25 to 50 inches (63.5 cm to 1.3 m) per year, with fruits such as olives at the drier end of that range and subtropicals such as avocados at the maximum. If rainfall isn't enough, evaluate the site's access to water and decide how the trees will be watered *before* planting them. See chapter 5, Irrigation and Fertilization, for help in making that decision. At the very least, all fruit trees will need a consistent water source in close proximity, such as from a spigot, for the first few years after planting as they become established. Test the distance by hooking up a hose (or series of hoses) to the nearest spigot to determine if there is enough water pressure to transport water directly to the planting site.

Above: Fruit trees should always be in proximity to a water source, such as a spigot, during times of drought and for the first few years after planting.

Below: Trees thrive near natural bodies of water as they draw on underground water resources, such as these trees on the banks of the Klamath River in California. You may not have a natural body of water in your yard, but you can use this same principle on properties with smaller flowing or standing water sources.

MANAGING MICROCLIMATES

Microclimates are subtle influences on temperature provided by landforms, manmade structures, or masses of tall trees (hedgerows, windbreaks, forests). Their influence causes changes in the movement of cold air through a site. They can be regional: differences in climate on one side of a mountain range versus the other, for example. They can be as small as a backyard, too. Cold air flows like water to the lowest spot. Midway up that gentle slope of those easy rolling hills is the perfect planting place for two reasons: better soil drainage and cold air flows on past, keeping frost from settling on trees. Being aware of and managing microclimates can benefit fruit trees by moderating temperature and using it to the best advantage.

Skillful strategies can be used to "stretch" local climate zone limits—to grow a fruit tree that needs a little warmer climate in a slightly cooler one, or the reverse.

- Sun-soaked walls and sidewalks collect heat all day and release that stored heat at night, protecting nearby vulnerable trees from frost damage.

- Low spots that collect cold air, as long as the soil drains well, can be used to maximize the chill needed to set the fruit of temperate zone trees such as apples and peaches.

- Look around your neighborhood for examples of thriving fruit trees and use nature as a guide to evaluate local microclimates and determine which types of trees will do well there.

Manipulating microclimates will not enable us to grow avocados on the Canadian plains, but can give a one half to one full USDA climate zone stretch (more on chill requirements and climate zones in the next chapter).

Use slopes to improve drainage and plant midway down the slope to protect sensitive trees, such as this citrus tree, from frost damage.

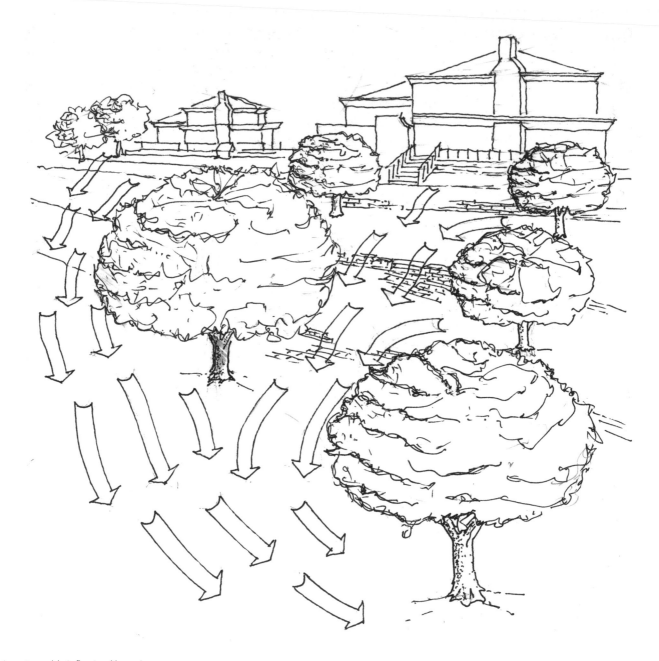

Imagine cold air flowing like water over the contours of a site in order to choose the appropriate spots for fruit trees. Remember that some temperate fruit trees require more chill in order to produce fruit.

PLANTING SOLUTIONS FOR SMALL OR URBAN SPACES

Alternative planting solutions for small, usually urban, sites include fruit tree hedgerows, multiple trees planted in a single planting hole, raised beds, and containers. Sunlight and air circulation requirements are the same for these types of plantings as for standard home orchards. All maintenance tasks—watering, fertilizing, pruning, and plant health care—need to be performed more frequently, although on a smaller scale, with these types of plantings.

Fruit Tree Hedgerows

Fruit tree hedgerows are linear thickets, with trees planted in 3-foot (0.9 m) intervals. Available space determines the length, but leave enough room (at least 24 inches, or 61 cm) to access the row from both sides and each end to perform maintenance. True dwarf or semi-dwarf rootstocks are recommended for fruit tree hedgerows, but trees on any rootstock will be stunted in this type of planting because of the intense competition for soil and sunlight resources. This results in a smaller harvest per tree, as well as smaller trees.

- Choose a maximum height for the hedgerow, between 6 to 12 feet (1.8 to 3.7 m), and maintain it with summer pruning.

- The space between individual trees must be maintained with pruning also, a minimum of 6 to 12 inches (15.2 to 30.5 cm).

- All individual trees in a fruit tree hedgerow should be pruned to a *modified central leader* shape. (Information on this fruit tree form is presented in the pruning section of chapter 6, Pruning and Weeding.)

Fruit tree hedgerows offer the chance to have an extended harvest of a variety of fruits from a small planting site. Since they are kept relatively short, harvest is also more accessible, especially for families wanting to pick fruit together.

Types of fruit suggested for this planting style are both the temperate zone fruits: apples, peaches, pears, and so on, and smaller subtropical fruits such as acerola cherry, jaboticaba, and Surinam cherry. Smaller citrus, like kumquat, may be attempted, but excellent air circulation around and through all types of citrus is essential for disease prevention.

Multiple Trees, One Planting Hole

Another option for planting in tight spaces includes planting multiple trees, from two to four, placed about 18 inches (45.7 cm) apart, in a single planting hole. This will also extend the fruit harvest from two or three weeks to two or three months. In the end, the trees are maintained as a single tree, managed as an *open-vase* shape (see chapter 6, Pruning and Weeding).

- Plant the same type of fruit trees together in one planting hole: three peaches, three apples, three avocados.

- For the temperate zone fruit trees, having the same rootstock for each tree is helpful, but plant different fruit varieties of each (see chapter 3, Plant Selection, for more on rootstocks).

- Extend the harvest by selecting an early-season, mid-season, and late-season variety of the same fruit.

- Competition stunts individual trees in this planting method, just like the fruit tree hedgerow, so each harvest will be smaller.

- Choose the same height for all the trees in the planting hole, and maintain it with pruning. The types of fruit trees recommended for hedgerows can also be planted this way, as well as avocados and figs.

- For citrus, consider choosing a single tree with multiple varieties grafted on rather than multiple trees in a hole.

If space is limited in backyards, trees may be planted close together and maintained with pruning to keep them from competing. These trees were planted close to each other, forming a fruit tree hedgerow.

Planting multiple trees per hole is another technique used to maximize quantities while keeping trees at a manageable height in tight quarters. These apricots were planted next to each other in the same planting hole along with other companion plants.

RAISED BEDS

Raised beds are mounds of planting medium placed on top of an existing soil. They may be enclosed with walls made of wood, rock, concrete block, or many other types of building materials. They may also simply be mounded on top of soil without any walls surrounding their edges. Raised beds are a quick fix used to sidestep problems such as poor drainage and shallow soil. They are typically used for smaller, nonwoody plants, such as vegetables and flowers, but can provide an opportunity to grow dwarf or semidwarf fruit trees.

A raised bed that may be used for a fruit tree must be at least 18 inches (45.7 cm) high, with a native soil below of at least the same depth.

For easy access, build a raised bed no wider than arm's length from the edge to the center of the bed. For example, for a person 6 feet (1.8 m) tall, a raised bed should be roughly 6 feet (1.8 m) wide, so reaching 3 feet (0.9 m) into the center from either side is comfortable.

Factor in the distance needed between mature fruit trees when determining the length of the bed, or place only one fruit tree per bed, with companion plants filling out the remainder.

Remember to estimate the width of mature fruit tree canopies overhead when determining the placement of multiple raised beds, side to side.

Concerns and Considerations

Raised beds provide a solution that comes at a price. Explore options to use recycled materials, and be aware of the limitations of wood. Wood is biodegradable and will gradually decompose, especially the side of the raised bed walls in contact with the planting medium. Scrap wood left over from the construction of structures has usually been treated with chemicals to resist decay. Some of these substances, arsenic for example, are toxic and leach out of the wood, into the soil, where they are taken up by plant roots. If choosing wood to build raised beds, try to get untreated, recycled wood.

Additional caution is advised when selecting a soil medium to fill raised beds.

- Avoid importing problems such as root-rot fungi, root-knot nematodes, or invasive plant seeds. Buy from a reputable dealer for bulk purchases.

- Try to choose a planting medium that is not dramatically unlike the native soil below—choose one that's better, but not *completely* different (doing so can negatively affect drainage; see chapter 4, Planting, for more on backfill).

- Till or fork the top 6 to 10 inches (15.2 to 25.4 cm) of the native soil right before placing the fill for the raised bed on top.

- Do not rake or smooth this tilled area before adding the fill. The goal here is to have tree roots extend into the native soil from the planting medium in the raised bed above.

Applying a layer of compost and mulch to the surface of the raised bed provides the same benefits as for plantings directly into the ground: namely, cooler soils that evaporate water from their surfaces more slowly, with fewer weeds. Irrigation for raised beds can be provided using any of the methods for watering fruit trees planted in the ground. Keep in mind, however, that raised beds drain more quickly and may need a more frequent irrigation schedule. Decide how the raised beds will be watered before building them (see chapter 5, Irrigation and Fertilization, for details.)

CONTAINER-GROWN TREES

Plants in pots bring joy to small spaces. Fruit trees grown in containers can offer a delicious harvest as well. Growing fruit trees in containers uses "unusable" space, fitting a tree where one would not before. Fruit trees grown in containers are much smaller than their counterparts in the ground and produce a smaller harvest. More maintenance is required to keep container-grown fruit trees thriving than for in-ground trees, but these tasks are easier to perform since the trees are smaller and portable.

Container culture of fruit trees enables us to enjoy fruits we might not be able to grow in the ground; citrus in cold-winter climates, for example. Containers can be moved indoors, to a greenhouse or sunny room, to wait out the winter. Back out on the patio for the warm seasons, fruit trees in containers bring their beauty closer to us, displaying normal-size fruit on miniature trees, at just about eye-level.

For best success, be sure to choose a fruit tree variety specifically bred for container culture. Not every type of fruit tree can be adapted to life in a planting pot, but the following list provides a variety of choices that are most readily available:

- ✓ Apples on M27 rootstock
- ✓ Genetic dwarf peaches and nectarines
- ✓ Cherries on Gisela rootstock
- ✓ Citrus on true dwarfing rootstock (trifoliate, "Flying Dragon")
- ✓ Figs
- ✓ Fruiting mulberries
- ✓ Pomegranates
- ✓ Loquats
- ✓ Olives

Choosing Your Container

Plant containers also come in a terrific variety of shapes and colors. When selecting a container for a fruit tree, include practical concerns along with aesthetic desires. A diameter of 20 to 24 inches (50.8 to 61 cm) is the minimum size needed for a container-grown fruit tree—and *always* give preference to recycled or previously owned materials.

Raised beds allow fruit trees to be grown in shallow, poor-quality soils.

Regular root pruning every three to five years for container-grown trees will prevent them from becoming root-bound and will extend their lives. Gently remove several inches of soil and roots away from the sides and bottom of the tree before returning to its container.

Wood is a popular pick for plant containers; half whiskey barrels are almost iconic. Wood gives a certain rustic look and doesn't heat up so rapidly in sunlight that tree roots get "cooked," but it does decompose quickly when in contact with soil and water. That half whiskey barrel, which wasn't cheap, may rot and collapse in a single growing season.

Another garden icon, *clay,* or *terra cotta*, pots are popular too, and often less expensive than wood. At the size needed to grow a fruit tree, however, a clay container can be heavy—even without potting mix, a tree, and water inside. Clay containers are porous and draw moisture out of the planting medium as they dry. They also heat up in sunlight, raising the soil temperature for tree roots. Once the pot and the potting mix dry out a little, a gap forms between them. Water tends to flow right through this space and out the drainage hole below, while the container's soil and the tree's roots are still dry. This can happen with any type of plant container that is not kept consistently moist, but it occurs more quickly with a clay plant pot.

Ceramic containers are clay pots that have been painted with a glaze and fired; they have a shiny, nonporous surface. Light colors can reflect heat away, keeping roots cooler. Ceramic plant containers can be highly ornamental, or very plain. Whatever their appearance, they are usually durable and long-lasting. They are also more expensive, typically heavy, and both cumbersome and fragile during maintenance tasks like root pruning.

Plastic containers have evolved in recent decades to look a lot better than they used to. Colors and shapes are available that mimic terra cotta and stone. They are lightweight, durable, much less fragile than ceramic or clay containers—and they don't rot like wood. Most of the time, they are less expensive than any of the other material types. Plastic does heat up in sunlight, though, to root-cooking temperatures. Choosing lighter colors, and placing trees to get their direct sun hours in the first part of the day, can help with this problem.

Soil and Water Considerations

Tree roots growing inside a container have a limited soil reservoir to draw moisture from; container culture of fruit trees demands more frequent watering than for in-ground trees. Water two or three times per week during the warmest season of the year, less often during the trees' dormant season, cool times of the year, or during time spent indoors. Remember that gap between the wall of the clay pot and the dry potting mix? Try to prevent that by keeping container-grown fruit trees evenly moist all of the time, without letting them get soggy.

A standard potting mix works well for container-grown fruit trees. Choose one that has both good drainage and good moisture retention properties. Commercially available mixes have both qualities and usually come prefertilized, but frequent watering makes short work of the nutrients included in a potting mix. Container-grown fruit trees need regular fertilization: monthly with a liquid, organic fertilizer. For all fruits except citrus, choose a low-nitrogen formula with micronutrients and calcium. More nitrogen is appropriate for citrus. For more details and information about fertilizers, see chapter 5, Irrigation and Fertilization.

Most container-grown fruit trees will need to be staked if they show signs of buckling under the weight of their fruit. Those stakes will need to stay on longer than for in-ground trees, and some container-grown fruit trees will need to be staked throughout their lives.

Pruning top growth should be limited for at least the first few years. It's already a very small tree; remove as little fruitwood as possible. Root pruning, however, must be performed every three to five years.

To Root Prune a Container Tree

Choose a cool, cloudy day, at the beginning of the growing season, well before bud break or bloom, but after the last frost.

1. Remove the tree from its container, and using a sharp spade or gardening knife, slice away 5 to 7 inches (12.7 to 17.8 cm) of roots and soil all the way around the root-ball, and across the bottom, too.

2. Put a layer of new potting soil in the bottom of the container, and replace the tree inside the container.

3. Fill in new potting soil around the perimeter of the container, and water the tree thoroughly.

This practice is very similar to the art of bonsai and lengthens the lives of container-grown fruit trees. Fruit trees grown in the ground still live much longer than those in containers, with fewer maintenance chores, to boot. But perhaps the chance to pick a fresh lemon when icicles dangle from the eaves is worth the struggle— and certainly better than no fruit tree at all.

Varieties that normally would not grow in certain climates can do well in containers. This citrus is portable, so it can come indoors during frosts.

chapter three

PLANT SELECTION

The tree is a human concept. Designating a plant as a tree, and not a shrub or a forb, is a definition based on consensus. We use it to help us sort out the multitude of plants growing in the world around us.

WE AGREE THAT A TREE IS A WOODY
perennial, with a dominant vertical trunk that
is taller than 15 feet (4.6 m).[20] Understanding
some basic facts about tree structure and
function assists in making good choices when
selecting fruit trees to plant at home.

FRUIT TREE BASICS: ROOTS AND SHOOTS

There's life underground. Roots perform four
major functions in the lives of trees:

- Absorb water and nutrients from the soil

- Anchor the tree to the ground

- Store carbohydrates (sugars) made by the
  leaves as an energy reserve

- Aid in the transport of water and nutrients
  up into and sugars down from the
  tree's trunk.

Roots also maintain symbiotic relationships with
microorganisms living in vibrant, healthy soils.

Ninety percent of tree roots live in the top 18
to 24 inches (45.7 to 61 cm) of soil because
that's where the oxygen is. Roots need oxygen,
just like we do. So, soggy soils, full of water,
and soils compacted by vehicle and foot traffic
are difficult environments for tree roots. Roots
spread out, not down. A few large anchoring
roots reach down below the oxygen zone of
the top 18 to 24 inches (45.7 to 61 cm), but a
broad net of roots, called a *root plate*, holds the
tree up, spreading out like a large dish with the
trunk jutting up out of the center. Tree roots
can spread out past the *dripline* (the ends of the
branches) and reach lateral widths from 1½ to
3 times the height of the tree.

The *root crown*, where a tree's tissues change
from roots to trunk (i.e., from the parts that
are supposed to be below ground to the parts
that are supposed to be above ground), should

be partially visible, right at soil level. The root
crown is a critical and vulnerable place on a tree
that must not be buried with soil or mulch at
planting. Burying the root crown shortens the
life span of trees and makes them more susceptible to disease.

Tree trunks are wider at their bases than in their
middle sections. Trunk *taper* helps trees endure
the force of wind. With time and maturity, trees
develop a flare at the bases of their trunks,
at the root crown. This *basal flare* should be
noticeable on mature trees.

A strong, healthy tree trunk supports the weight
of all the tree's branches, twigs, leaves, and fruit.
It endures, absorbs, and moves down into the

2 ft. (0.6 m)

Above: Tree roots are not
a mirror image of the trunk
and branches. They grow
laterally, mostly in the top 2
feet (0.6 m) of soil.

Opposite page: Sometimes
there is a fine line between
the definitions of trees
and shrubs, and one can
become the other based on
growth and maintenance.
This serviceberry can be
grown as a large shrub or
pruned into a small tree.

[20] Harris, R.W., N. Matheny and J. Clark. 2004. *Arboriculture: Integrated Management of Landscape Trees, Shrubs and Vines*. (Prentice Hall: Upper Saddle River, N.J.).

Basal flare, also known as trunk flare, provides support and becomes more pronounced as a tree ages. The flare on this trunk is from an eight-year-old peach tree.

ground the physical stress of carrying that load under the action of wind. Tree trunks should be straight, without doglegs, and should stand straight up, without significant lean.

Round for a Reason

Trunks are round for a reason; both mechanical engineers and trees know that the cylinder is a strong form, even when hollow. Hollow trees can persist and survive weather events for a long time, even though they have suffered significant decay. Ultimately, solid tree trunks are stronger than hollow ones, so choose trunks that are round, without flat spots, big cracks, or hollows.

Trees have two crowns. Above the root crown, the sum total of branches, twigs, and leaves is called the *crown*, or the *canopy*. For clarity, the terms *root crown* and *canopy* will be used throughout this book. A fruit tree has all of the structures just described—roots, root crown, trunk, and canopy—performing the same functions as any other type of tree. Most commercially grown fruit trees, however, are really two trees in one, as described below.

ROOTSTOCKS

For more than two thousand years, since the Hellenistic period, rootstocks have been used for the propagation of fruit trees.[21] The combination of *rootstock* and *fruitwood*, in a practice called *grafting*, is used to create fruit trees that have it all: vigorous root systems that resist disease and control tree height, grafted to trees with dense, lush foliage, which are resistant to a different array of diseases than the rootstock and produce tasty fruits. In other words, roots that are known to be strong and hardy are fused together with the fruitwood of a tree known to produce high-quality fruit by splicing and joining the two together. Otherwise, just as offspring from the same parents can have different characteristics, strengths, and weaknesses in the animal kingdom, growing fruit trees from seeds results in unpredictable tree varieties that often produce little to no fruit of a lesser quality. Grafting allows growers to offer fruit trees with known qualities.

Vigor

The backyard fruits most commonly grown today are the result of plant breeding processes called *hybridization*, which tends to diminish

[21] Webster, A.D. 2010 Mar 22. "Temperate fruit tree rootstock propagation." *New Zealand Journal of Crop and Horticultural Science.*

some qualities of the original, wild trees, such as a vigorous root system, in favor of others, like larger fruits with sweeter flavors. Plants have a finite amount of energy available to distribute among the functions they need to complete. Rootstocks are selected to provide the vigor that the root systems of hybridized trees, bred for fruit quality, cannot supply for themselves anymore. Sometimes rootstocks are simply random seedlings of the same species as the fruitwood. Wild avocado saplings, for example, make a good platform to graft on other avocado fruitwood varieties like Haas or Fuerte.

Disease Resistance

After vigor, many rootstocks are selected for their ability to resist the diseases or insect attacks most common to a type of fruit tree, or to the soil it grows in. Nemaguard rootstock, used for nectarines, apricots, plums, and almonds, is resistant to root-knot nematodes: microscopic worms that bore into plant roots, crippling them and stunting the whole plant. This rootstock also has a reputation for vigor but doesn't have outstanding tolerance for poorly draining soils.

Height Management

Rootstocks offer another category of benefits in height management of the mature fruit tree. The terms *true-dwarf*, *semidwarf*, and *standard* describe the influence of a rootstock on the growth rate of the fruitwood. The term *genetic dwarf* refers to a fruitwood variety with a diminutive stature of its own, regardless of the rootstock.

Standard rootstocks produce full-size trees, apple trees that reach 30 to 40 feet (9.1 to 12.2 m), for example. Commercial agriculture typically uses standard rootstocks. Semidwarf rootstocks, widely available in retail garden centers, reduce the overall mature height of fruit trees from 50 to 75 percent of standard rootstocks. The total height varies, depending on the type of fruit tree, but most semidwarfs top out at around 15 to 20 feet (4.6 to 6.1 m).

Along with pruning and maintenance, rootstocks determine the mature size of a fruit tree. From top to bottom, we see a progression of dwarfing to standard-size trees.

| True dwarf | Semidwarf | Standard |

True-dwarf rootstocks produce mature trees at a height of 5 to 7 feet (1.5 to 2.1 m). Normal-size fruit is borne on tiny trees that begin to fruit early, two to four years old, and fruit most heavily from about eight to twelve years old. Suitable for planting in the backyard, or growing in containers, true-dwarf fruit trees keep maintenance and harvesting chores within arm's reach, usually without a ladder. For example, Flying Dragon, a selection of trifoliate orange (*Poncirus trifoliata*), keeps citrus trees at just 5 to 7 feet (1.5 to 2.1 m) tall by twelve to thirteen years old. Trees grown in containers are even smaller on this rootstock. Flying Dragon also imparts some resistance to root rot and an increased tolerance of cold temperatures.[22]

Many rootstocks supply all three categories of benefits simultaneously: vigor, disease resistance, and size reduction, with additional bonuses like acceptance of adverse soil conditions. Those that do not can be grafted with an interstock, a second variety of rootstock, grafted between the first rootstock and the fruitwood, to maximize benefits available from the most popular rootstocks.

22 Ferguson, J. and T. M. Spann. 2010. Publication #HS982, University of Florida, IFAS Extension.

Choose fruit trees on rootstocks that have characteristics that address planting site conditions and long-term maintenance goals. For example, in tight, urban areas, choose dwarfing varieties; to create backyard shade for summertime recreational spaces, pick standards.

Above: For grafted fruit trees, height at maturity is determined by the rootstock: true-dwarf, semidwarf, or standard (depicted left to right), all of which can produce significant harvests. Though at lesser per tree yields than standards, dwarfed trees often produce fruit at a younger age and can be planted more densely. Due to their larger size, standards provide the greatest benefit for the environment.

Below: Check nursery tags for both rootstock (pink label in this photo) and fruitwood (white label) to understand the full profile of the fruit tree. Often, information for both is contained on a single label.

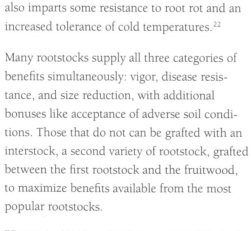

FRUITWOOD

Moving up from roots to shoots, let's talk about the qualities of fruitwood (also known as a *scion* when grafted to a rootstock), or the portion of the tree above the graft union. First off, the fruitwood determines the fruit type: for example, an apple, orange, pear, or plum. Next, the fruitwood is a *variety* or *cultivar*: for example, a specific plum, bred to have certain characteristics of color, taste, size, and texture. Varieties occur as natural variations of a fruit type; cultivars are produced as a result of plant breeding efforts. Most fruitwoods offered are cultivars, but the two terms are used interchangeably. Varieties and cultivars are designated with names, often trademarked. In the plant name *Prunus persica Bonanza II*, the term *Bonanza II* is the cultivar name for this genetic dwarf peach. Typically, there are many cultivars to choose from for each fruit type; for example, the apple alone has up to 20,000 named cultivars in existence.[23]

Fruitwood is bred and selected first for fruit quality: size, color, and taste, but also for attributes like fruit "holding" well on the tree, or *self-thinning*—dropping some immature fruit to produce fewer, larger fruits, as opposed to many, smaller ones. The fruitwood varieties bred for home orchards also focus on regional adaptation. Apple varieties best for backyards in New England are not the same as those created for the American Southwest, Middle East, or other arid climates. Resistance to both foliar and fruit diseases is also an important quality for fruitwood. (See chapter 7, Prevention, Troubleshooting, and Controls, for more information on common fruit tree maladies.)

[23] Juniper, B.E. and D.J. Mabberley. 2006. *The Story of the Apple*. (Timber Press, Inc.: Portland, Ore.).

These two plums are growing side-by-side, but they are different cultivars based on their fruitwood, and they produce fruits with different characteristics, such as size, color, and taste.

DAYS TO HARVEST

Days to harvest, the next characteristic of fruitwood we'll examine, refers to the number of days from bloom to ripe fruit. As a rule of thumb, for successful backyard fruit tree culture, 150 days between first and last frost is the minimum for fruit production.[24] Days to harvest lengths are grouped into early, mid-season, and late. *Early* fruit tree cultivars, bred for regions with the shortest growing seasons, produce mature fruit in the fewest number of days. When *mid-season* occurs depends on where the trees grow, late June through July for the southern United States, but late July through August for the northern states. Some *late* season cultivars are bred for fruit qualities best for canning or freezing, to facilitate storing over the winter months. Some fruits, such as persimmons, ripen in late season naturally. Research different cultivars to determine which will provide fruits at a time most desired by those in the household.

[24] Delmas, R. 2003. "Growing Tree Fruit at Home." Fact Sheet #2-03, University of California Cooperative Extension.

GRAFT UNIONS

Fruitwood from one tree and rootstock from another join together at the *graft union*, a splice connecting wood from the two. The resulting tree has the best qualities of both plants. The graft union is a wound, sometimes sealed with a paste, usually wrapped in tape, until it heals. For a graft union to be successful, the rootstock and the fruitwood must be compatible, meaning that the two plants typically come from the same *genus*, or at least from the same plant family. Grafting an apple fruitwood onto a citrus rootstock won't work. Other factors come into play after this basic requirement is met, and sometimes, graft unions are not happy ones.

Graft unions that are healthy look relatively smooth, making a clean, uniform transition from rootstock to fruitwood. One stem may be

Fruit Trees or Time Machines?

Choose cultivars that are known to thrive in the planting site's region and produce a type of fruit that you and your friends and family enjoy eating most. Consider heirloom or heritage fruit trees, which are antique varieties from earlier periods of human history that have remained unchanged for decades to centuries through genetic preservation. Many heirloom varieties offer superior flavor, nutrition, and a connection to a time when trees were grown without synthetic pesticides or poisons. Choosing heirloom varieties also helps preserve genetic diversity.

Look for a smooth transition at the graft union from rootstock to fruitwood when selecting a fruit tree.

a little thicker than the other, but the difference should not be dramatic. A graft union with an unusually large swelling, a separate bumpy growth on the side of the union, or any type of ooze dripping out is showing signs of incompatibility. Avoid purchasing and planting trees with unhealthy graft unions. Incompatible graft unions shorten tree life spans, sometimes to just ten to fifteen years, and increase the risk of structural failure, like the tree snapping off at the graft union.

The graft union should be healed by the time the tree is offered for sale, but it will always be a little vulnerable. Try to face the graft union away from the dominant direction of the sun when planting a fruit tree. Exactly where the graft union sits on the trunk varies from tree to tree, but it is usually well above the root crown. Do not bury the graft union when planting a fruit

tree or mistake it for the root crown and plant the tree too deep. Any leafy growth that sprouts at or below the graft union will be the rootstock, and therefore a different variety of tree than the fruitwood, and should be removed. The rootstock plant's leaves may look very different from the fruitwood's foliage, making it easy to discern.

POLLINATION

Pollination is the plant process that begins the transformation of flowers into fruit. Fruit starts as a swelling at the base of a pollinated flower; after the petals fall away, the fruit continues to grow to its full size and ripens. When pollination doesn't happen, no fruit forms after the flower fades. Knowing a little something about the pollination requirements of fruit trees makes the difference between having a backyard full of fruit, or not.

A *perfect* (hermaphroditic) flower has both pollen (male parts) and the structures that receive pollen and form seeds (female parts). A perfect flower may or may not be capable of pollinating itself. Fruit tree cultivars that have flowers able to receive their own pollen and set fruit are called *self-fruitful*. Most citrus are self-fruitful, as are most peaches, nectarines, apricots, and sour cherries.

In general, fruit set is enhanced by planting more than one of each tree, even if listed as self-fruitful, so consider planting multiple trees.

Some fruit trees are *self-unfruitful*. Their flowers are perfect, but they need pollen from another cultivar of the same fruit type to pollinate their flowers and set fruit. Apples, pears, and sweet cherries typically need *cross-pollination*. To achieve this, pollinizer trees should be planted in close proximity, within 100 to 200 feet (30.5 to 61 m), but the closer the better—more like within 50 feet (15.2 m) in a backyard setting. Other cross-pollination techniques include grafting pollinizer branches onto trees or planting multiple trees in a hole.

Timing

Sometimes it's a matter of timing. Avocados are self-fruitful, but some trees have flowers ready to receive pollen in the morning, with pollen

All fruits begin as flowers. Insects, birds, and wind act as pollinators and are essential for fruit set. Some trees need other cultivars in order to cross-pollinate, so check labels to learn exactly which partner tree is needed, if any.

that isn't released until the afternoon of the next day (Type A). Other avocados display the opposite pattern: flowers ready in the afternoon, with pollen released the following morning (Type B). Avocado fruit set is improved with a planting of both Type A and B trees. Bananas, oriental persimmon, and navel oranges set fruit without any pollination at all.

Pollen is built to travel; the tiny, lightweight grains float in the air and migrate on a breeze. Nut trees, self-unfruitful, are primarily wind-pollinated. But sometimes the wind doesn't get you where you want to go. Pollen is also pretty sticky and gloms onto bee backs and hummingbird beaks really well. Plants spend their precious energy, sometimes up to 15 percent, to make their flowers look pretty, smell great, and taste sweet—just to get their pollen carried around. Pollinators, like honeybees, other insects, and hummingbirds, are very important contributors to fruit set. Citrus are mostly self-fruitful, but numerous studies have shown that fruit set is increased when honeybees are at work in the groves. Insect-pollinated citrus fruits are also larger, juicer, and have more seeds. Most self-fruitful trees benefit with increased fruit set in the presence of pollinators.

Weather Report

Weather affects pollination. Rain at the wrong time can spoil fruit tree blooms and splash pollen down into the mud below. Bees do not fly on cold, overcast, rainy, or very windy days. Late frosts can kill fruit tree flowers and tiny new fruits outright. Pollination and fruit set varies from year to year, affecting the total harvest.

Check nursery tags on fruit trees to determine if they are self-fruitful or self-unfruitful, the latter of which will typically list cultivars to cross-pollinate with. Online research will also reveal a more exhaustive listing of compatible cultivars for cross-pollination. In either case, consider planting multiple trees of that type to maximize fruit set and quality.

Fruit Tree Intelligence

Turns out, fig trees are quite smart—and sticklers for contracts. Eighty million years ago, fig trees and fig wasps entered into a symbiotic relationship where the wasps were allowed to lay their eggs inside a fig tree's nutrient-filled fruit in exchange for gathering and spreading fig pollen to other trees. Researchers at the Smithsonian Tropical Research Institute found that when wasps broke the agreement and failed to gather any pollen, yet still laid their eggs, the tree punished those particular wasps by dropping the fruit and preventing their eggs from hatching. After all, pollination is indeed serious business, and a deal is a deal, especially one that is millions of years old![25]

[25] Jander C. K. and E. A. Herre. 2010 Jan 13. "Host sanctions and pollinator cheating in the fig tree-fig wasp mutualism." *Proc. R. Soc. B.*

CHILL HOURS AND CLIMATE

Temperate zone fruit trees need the winter's cold. How much, and for how long, has been quantified by researchers and labeled with the moniker, *chill hours*. What's a chill hour? Basically, a chill hour is measured as a full hour at temperatures between 32°F and 45°F (0°C and 7°C). Some methods count hours with any temperature below 45°F (7°C), and others add and subtract for hours below 45°F (0°C) and above 60°F (15.5°C).[26]

[26] Byrne, D. H. and T. A. 1992. Bacon. "Chilling Accumulation: Its Importance & Estimation." Dept. of Horticultural Sciences, Texas A&M University.

Cold temperatures that are not below freezing help temperate zone fruit trees prepare for still colder days to come in the depths of winter. Chill hours help the trees to go dormant. Temperate zone fruit trees form leaf and flower buds during summertime for the next year. These buds need a dormant period first in order to grow normally later, when the spring comes. Warm spells, with temperatures above 60°F (15.5°C), can reverse chill hours and delay the onset of dormancy. However, once enough chill hours have accumulated, and the trees become dormant, the occasional warm winter day will not cause trees to break out of

Certain fruit tree types and cultivars actually require cold weather in order to properly set fruit. These pears would not have such a harvest if they were planted in warm-winter regions, which require low-chill varieties.

dormancy prematurely. See the table below for a general understanding on the average number of chill hours needed for some common fruit types. There's a wide range for each fruit type because of variability among different cultivars and varieties.

Fruit type	Average chill hours required to set fruit
Apples	900–1000
Cherries	800–1200
Peaches	600–900
Plums	500–900
Apricots	350–900

Low-chill temperate zone fruit trees were developed for those home orchardists in warm-winter climates not content with their paradise of citrus, avocado, and other subtropical fruits. These cultivars can achieve dormancy, and ultimately fruit set, with a minimum of chill hours. With the exception of sweet cherries, most temperate zone fruit types have low-chill cultivars available. These low-chill trees do not fare well in cold winter areas; they tend to lose blooms and early fruit set to late frosts.

The result of planting a fruit tree requiring more chill hours than a region's winter supplies is a bigger disappointment, though; the tree probably won't set fruit at all. Trees short on chill hours are slow to unfurl new leaves when spring does come. These late leaves tend to be clustered in puffs at the ends of branches; some foliage may even sprout from the trunk. Flowers will be small, flattened, or misshapen, and unable to set fruit at all.

Leave chill hour calculations to the researchers, but find out the average for the orchard site's region and compare that to the cultivar being considered. Check with the local Agricultural Extension or Master Gardener's program to find out the region's chill hours and which temperate zone fruit tree cultivars are best for your area.

Climate maps showing which regions are appropriate for certain fruit types and cultivars are easily accessible online through World Hardiness Zones maps; or obtain additional climate information through local nurseries and Agricultural Extension agents. In the U.S., the USDA's Plant Hardiness Zone Map is one resource that can be used to determine the planting site's zone and compare it to that of which a particular cultivar is known to grow well, in order to get a general sense of what might be possible in your backyard (see Recommended Reading section).

SELECTING FRUIT TREES

Now, armed with a bounty of useful knowledge—about both the site conditions, as well as the structure and needs of fruit trees—it's time to decide which cultivars to plant. Having a tree full of fruit is very different than picking up a few at the grocery. Which fruits do you, and the whole household, enjoy enough to have an entire harvest of? Pick favorite fruit types, and then begin to learn about the cultivars that will meet your needs and the site's demands most effectively. Two checklists are offered on page 52 to help sort things out, and don't hesitate to ask local experts which fruit tree cultivars are the best for your area.

Site Factors:

✓ Average rainfall

✓ Average sunlight

✓ Average chill hours received

✓ Growing season (frost-free days)

✓ Soil drainage

✓ Air circulation

✓ Total available planting space

✓ Pre-existing problems: nematodes, compacted soil, etc.

Tree Factors:

✓ Favorite fruit types

✓ Tree size: true-dwarf, semidwarf, standard

✓ Chill hours required

✓ Cross-pollination cultivars needed

✓ Special vulnerabilities to diseases

With a clear fruit tree planting plan in mind, it's time to find fruit trees. Purchasing a quality tree prevents struggle and disappointment in the weeks, sometimes years, after it is planted. A quality tree is free of significant defects in its roots and shoots. It has achieved a normal size for its age and species. Its foliage shows good color and density, without evidence of damage caused by insects or disease. Not least of all, a quality tree actually is the cultivar it's labeled to be.

Trunks

When arborists refer to the trunk of a sapling, we use the term *central leader*. Take a good look at the central leader of a young fruit tree for sale. Is it growing up straight? Is the bark smooth and clean-looking, without many pruning scars? Has the tree been *topped*? Nurseries often cut central leaders on young trees to encourage side branches to sprout. This practice makes the trees a little bushier and more attractive to customers. Topping, however, has long-

term consequences for the future mature trees. Look first for trees that have not been topped; as a second choice, look for a new stem sprouting near the top that appears thick and upright enough to be trained as a new central leader. This is necessary for trees that will be pruned into a modified central leader form. The impact of topping is less significant for trees that will be maintained in an open-vase shape. Check the graft union. Make sure, first of all, that it hasn't been buried along with the root crown. Look for signs of incompatibility between the rootstock and the fruiting wood.

Branches

Examine the branches; there may not be many. Check for damage like breaks or bark tears. Look to see if the branches are spaced somewhat evenly around the central leader. Check the angle where each branch meets the central leader. A good range is 45 to 60 degrees; these are strong branch attachments. Narrower angles are weaker, but that does not mean that branches should be removed. For small branches on saplings, a spreader (a small piece of wood) can be placed to gradually train the branch and widen that angle. Branches with a diameter greater than half that of the central leader may develop into structural defects later; keep an eye on branches that want to be trunks someday. They will need to be pruned or removed entirely in the future (more on that in chapter 6, Pruning and Weeding).

Leaves

For fruit trees in leaf, is the foliage color, size, and density normal for the tree type? Are the leaves spaced well throughout the canopy? Clumps of leaves that look like poodle tails, foliage clustered at the ends of branches, can be an indication of stress or herbicide damage. Examine leaves for signs of insects or disease.

pawpaw

noni

papaya

jackfruit

persimmon

fig

loquat

pomegranate

chestnut

tamarind

jujube

cacao fruit

cacao tree

olive

Get Exotic!

Think outside the box when selecting fruit and nut trees. While the most common tree types may be popular for a reason—because they produce delicious fruit—variety is also the spice of life, so research what else grows in your region. Subtropical zones have plenty of amazing options, yet even colder climates can grow more than just apples, pears, and the like. Ever hear of a pawpaw tree, a cold-tolerant relative of the tropical cherimoya? Did you know that chocolate (cacao) grows on a fruit tree? There are thousands of fruit tree types and cultivars; experiment with new fruits you might not otherwise have access to. Check local nurseries or mail-order catalogs for organic trees, or go back in history with heirloom varieties.

Fruit

If the tree has fruit, check it over using the same criteria as that used to examine the leaves, and remove all of it after purchasing and before planting the tree. This allows the tree to use its energy to recover from transplant shock and begin growing new roots rather than expending it on producing fruit, and also prevents young tree branches from being weighted down into poor angles.

Roots

Examine the roots, too, even on a containerized tree; it can be done without damaging the root-ball. Ask for assistance from nursery personnel to help with getting a look at the outside of the root-ball. For containerized trees, first take a look at the surface of the potting mix inside the container for weeds (a well-kept tree will not have any). Next, look at the base of the central leader for lateral roots that should be

When selecting trees, look for smooth, clean trunks with a strong, straight central leader, well-angled branches, healthy, well-distributed leaves, and roots that are not overgrown or root-bound in their containers. This newly planted loquat tree and containerized apple tree display many desirable characteristics to warrant selection.

at soil level—not little hairlike white roots, but roots about half to whole pencil thickness for a tree in a size #5 container (often referred to as a 5-gallon container). Don't see any? Gently move potting mix away from around the central leader until you do, or until you've dug down so deeply that you give up. This will reveal if, or how much, the tree is planted too deeply in the container. Ideally, the first lateral roots will be near the surface of the soil.

After finding some lateral roots, look at their direction of growth. Check for roots that are tightly circling the base of the central leader, or are severely kinked. Circling roots on containerized trees are common, but there shouldn't be any before the roots hit the walls of the container—and those should just be the tiny, fibrous ones. If a tree has been properly root pruned each time it was transplanted to a larger size container, circling lateral roots can be avoided. Circling and girdling roots, and planting too deeply, kills many, many trees.

New little roots growing around the edge of the root-ball should be white or yellow and flexible. Black doesn't look good on tree roots, and dry and brittle doesn't either. A rotten egg–type or other bad smell indicates the presence of root rot. Do not purchase containerized trees infected with root rot.

Trees should not be root-bound in their containers. Smaller roots may be circling, but large roots the width of a pencil or greater that do so are an indication the tree has been in its container too long. If the tree does not slide out of its container after the sides have been pounded, this may also be an indication that the tree is root-bound. These pictures show a healthy root-ball (top) followed by progressive degrees of root-boundedness (with some soil washed away to expose the condition).

Healthy root-ball

Onset of circling roots

Root-bound

TREE SIZE

What size containerized tree is the best one to buy? Bigger isn't always better, but it is almost always more expensive. Time really is money in the nursery industry. Trees held for longer periods, to grow to a larger size, use more water and materials, and require more labor hours to maintain. For example, a typical retail price for a fruit tree in a size #5 container (often referred to as a 5-gallon container) is about half of one in a size #15 container (or 15-gallon), and about one-tenth the price of a 24-inch (61 cm) box tree. Larger sizes of containerized fruit trees on true-dwarfing rootstocks will be even more expensive because of their slow growth rates.

Young Trees

Younger trees grow more vigorously, and show an increased ability to adapt to site conditions more quickly than trees planted at a larger size. For fruit trees on standard or semidwarf rootstocks, the difference in size between a size #15 container (often referred to as a 15-gallon container) and a 24-inch (61 cm) box averages out to one to two years of growing time. After five years in the ground, the trees planted at a smaller size often outperform the larger specimens. Bigger isn't better for the tree, either. Planting a larger tree means digging a bigger planting hole. Smaller root-balls are easier to keep consistently moist after planting, which is critical for the tree's immediate survival. Larger-size trees have been grown in containers for a longer time. They've been "bumped," transplanted to progressively larger-size containers, more times, giving them more opportunities to develop significant root defects.

B&Bs

Balled and burlapped (B&B) trees are field-grown and have less chance of harboring serious root defects. Prepurchase examination of a B&B's root-ball will not be possible, but be sure to take a good look and perform any needed root pruning at planting time. Note that B&B trees are quite heavy and often require professional delivery and placement at the planting site.

FTPF has found that size #5 containers, such as those pictured here, or bareroot trees, offer the best combination of survivability and enough size to provide a head start for the tree. Unless there is a high vandalism risk, where smaller trees might be more susceptible, don't hesitate to choose them.

Bareroot Trees

Bareroot trees are also field-grown and display fewer root defects; they are almost always topped, however. If they are not prewrapped at the nursery, examining the roots will be simple. The little white "feeder" roots will not be present, but check the lateral roots. They should be well-spaced, not all growing on one side, not broken, and not feel dry or brittle. Some bareroot trees are packaged; their roots are encased in moist sawdust and wrapped in plastic. Bareroot trees should be planted as soon as possible. Those not planted immediately must be *heeled in*. Heeling in is a way to store bareroot plants temporarily, keeping their roots protected and moist, without actually planting them (see the Storage on page 58).

TREE TRANSPORT

After trees are selected and purchased, they must be transported to the orchard site. You have to get them home, in other words. For large orders, or large trees, consider having them delivered; it may be well worth the fee. Opportunities abound to damage and dry out new trees on the trip from the nursery to the backyard.

- To load them onto a vehicle, position the container against the inside end of the truck bed—root-ball against the cab wall. Use the same direction for minivans, SUVs, station wagons, and so on.

- Always pick up trees and plants by grasping the container, not the trunk. When possible, put one hand under the bottom of the container for support.

- Use more than one person to pick up and load each tree if needed.

- Be careful not to break branches.

- Trees can be laid down horizontally in the truck bed. Use wood blocks, rolled-up burlap or carpeting, bags of potting soil, *something* on either side of each container to keep the trees from rolling around while being transported.

A Family Affair!

Fruit trees are a long-term investment, so involve those who will benefit from the harvest most—children. Tell them that these trees will provide fruit for decades, for their children, and their children's children. Time and again, FTPF finds that youth are so excited to take part in all phases of the planting process, including tree selection and transport. In Brazil, our team arrived in the low-income village of Igarai to donate trees to each household and help with backyard plantings. Soon after our arrival, a throng of children formed around us, enthusiastically helping their families choose and carry trees to their new homes. Decades from now, they'll be able to point to those trees and talk about the legacy they helped create that day. Not many acts in a lifetime are as long-lasting and profound as planting fruit trees, so involve the young ones from the outset of the process by asking them to help select trees that will provide their favorite fruits. As a result, they will have the experience and inspiration to replicate the process on their own later in life and plant more trees!

Avoid carrying a tree by its trunk. Instead grab the sides of the container. When removed from the container, always keep one hand underneath the rootball for support.

- Keeping foliage inside the vehicle is the best way to prevent wind damage, but for trees in the back of an open truck bed, wrap leaves and branches with burlap, lightweight canvas, or plastic (use plastic only if it's not hot and the trip's not very far).

- Try to keep speeds below 45 mph, which is when wind damage starts to occur, and avoid high-speed routes.

- If the trees' canopies extend past the end of the truck bed, keep the tailgate lowered and attach red ribbon or tape to the end of the covered foliage to alert drivers behind.

On the way, look in the rearview mirror now and again to be sure the trees are staying put. If the load shifts, so that branches may be damaged, pull off when possible and correct the situation.

STORAGE

Once home, unload the trees immediately, just as carefully as they were loaded. Will the trees be planted right away? If not, store them out of the sun and wind. Water containerized trees.

To Heel in Bareroot Trees:

1. Shovel out a shallow, angled trench in a sheltered, shady spot. Exposure to sun and wind will dry out roots and shoots.

2. Lay the bareroot trees down with their roots in the trench; the trunks should extend up and out at an angle that keeps the branches off the ground.

3. Cover the roots *completely* with moist sawdust, soil, or a combination of both, then lightly water, but do not tamp down around the roots. Work quickly, so roots are not exposed for long. Leaving bareroot plants heeled in for lengthy periods is not recommended, but if they will not be planted for several days, the root covering may need to be lightly watered again. Keep the roots moist, but not soggy.

Heel bareroot trees in if they are not being planted immediately by digging a shallow, angled trench in a shaded area and covering the roots with a moist substrate such as soil or sawdust.

—chapter four—

PLANTING

When is the best time of year to plant fruit trees? For the most part, spring or autumn: spring for cold-winter climates; autumn for warm-winter and arid climates. Autumn and spring have cooler air temperatures (but not too cold), and the soil is still warm or warming up. This decreases heat stress for foliage, while providing below-ground conditions that favor root growth. Newly planted trees need to spend at least their first growing season, and preferably two or three, growing a strong, vibrant root system.

TIMING THE PLANTING

Spring is an excellent season to shop for fruit trees at local nurseries. For many regions, winter and early spring is the only time of year when bareroot fruit trees are available for purchase. Containerized trees are usually in stock year-round, but they tend to decrease in price, quality, and quantity as the year progresses, with "leftovers" remaining by late autumn. This may present an opportunity to plant more trees for your household, or perhaps as part of a community project, as it is a good time to approach nurseries about heavy discounts and possible donations to community plantings.

[27] Postman, J. 2003. "The Endicott Pear Tree—Oldest Living Fruit Tree in North America." Pomona 36:13–15. As of the publication of this book, the tree is still alive.

The oldest living fruit tree in North America is a pear. The tree is named the Endicott Pear Tree, after the first governor of Massachusetts, and is believed to have been shipped to the colonies from England in 1630.[27] This tree has endured hurricanes, vandalism, and the simple passage of time. It was already more than 140 years old when the Declaration of Independence was signed; it was first proclaimed by the government to be "old" in 1852. The Endicott Pear Tree is still producing fruit nearly 400 years later—but it wouldn't have survived its first decade had it not been planted correctly.

Plant trees in the spring or autumn, ideally, or at any time when there's enough room in your schedule to ensure the best level of aftercare. You can plant trees with success in a variety of conditions, as long as the ground isn't frozen or about to freeze.

This tree was planted during the hottest part of a summer day and suffered as a result. Always plan your summer plantings to take place during the coolest time of day and provide plenty of water to the trees afterward.

Truly, trees may be planted just about any time of the year—as long as the ground is not frozen. Frozen soil is tough to dig a hole into, and the expansion of soil as it freezes (called *heaving*) can readily toss up that tree you just planted. Planting trees in the heat of summer means keeping a close watch for wilting leaves and more frequent watering. Soil drainage must be very good to sharp for a summer planting to prevent root rots from attacking the new trees in the warm, wet soil. For a summertime planting, pick a cool day, and the coolest time of the day. In areas where irrigation is scarce, plant just before the rainy season.

SPOTTING THE LAYOUT

During the site selection process, spacing for new fruit trees and approximate locations for each were decided, but now that the trees are here, in the backyard, waiting to be planted, *spot* them out before digging the first hole. Place each tree in its chosen location, step back, and take a look. Carry the trees by holding the edges of the container, not the trunk. If planting bareroot trees, remember to *heel them in* (lean them to one side, and lightly but completely cover the bare roots with some moist soil, straw, or sawdust) or use another type of marker to stand in their place. Feel free to leave the trees in their spots for a day or two; just remember to water them in the meantime, while fine-tuning the whole arrangement. Think in future terms by pacing or measuring off probable mature canopy widths to help with imagining the trees fully grown with branches overhead. Consider how leaves and fruit may fall when planting near structures or social areas.

TOOLS

A pointed spade shovel and a hose connected to a spigot are the bare minimum tools needed to plant fruit trees. Mulching new trees at planting time prevents weed growth and conserves moisture in the soil; 2 cubic feet (56.6 L) of mulching material per tree is a good amount to start with. Half a cubic foot (14.2 L) of organic compost is optional but will provide a boost for the tree when applied topically. If the site contains heavy or compacted soils, a pickax will make it easier to loosen soil prior to digging. If the trees are root-bound, use a pair of pruners to free thick, circling roots. Root pruning will also be covered in chapter 6, Pruning and Weeding. A bow rake comes in handy and is a favorite tool to shape berms and smooth mulch around the base of a tree. If the trees require staking, two posts, a post pounder, and a tying material will be needed.

Planting Materials Checklist:

- ✓ Spade shovel (a)
- ✓ Water source (b)
- ✓ Mulch (c)
- ✓ Organic compost
- ✓ For heavy soils: Pickax (d)
- ✓ For root-bound trees: Pruners (e)
- ✓ For shaping berms and mulch: Bow rake (f)
- ✓ For staking: Two 4-foot (1.2 m) -long posts, post driver, and tying material

A tree may be successfully planted with just a spade shovel, irrigation, and mulch under many conditions. Often, the additional tools shown here are useful.

SITE PREPARATION

Grasses and other vegetation compete with a young tree for water, nutrients, and sometimes sunlight, so remove them from each planting spot. Stand where the tree will be planted, extending one arm out, parallel to the ground, and eyeball a circle of this radius around the planting hole (at least 4 feet, or 1.2 m, in diameter). This is the area that should be cleared.

Do not dig down deep during the clearing; this removes precious topsoil. Instead, place the shovel blade almost parallel to the ground, and skim the vegetation off 1 inch (2.5 cm) or so below the soil's surface. Break up any clods to retain that soil, and place the discarded vegetation in a pile for composting. Do not use the litter to backfill the tree hole.

REMOVING VEGETATION

When removing vegetation, stay low to the ground with one hand placed on the top of the shovel handle, pushing the blade straight through 1 to 2 inches (2.5 to 5.1 cm) below the soil.

Remove grass and vegetation in a wide-diameter circle to create a noncompetitive environment for the fruit tree to be planted—about as wide as when standing in the center of the circle with arms extended.

Planting Hole

The old gardener's saying goes, "Don't put a five-dollar plant into a fifty-cent hole." For trees, the value of digging planting holes the correct way and placing those trees correctly in them cannot be underestimated. Trees planted too deeply fail to thrive and live much shorter lives. Dig the planting hole to the depth of the root-ball in the container *and no deeper*—that means to the top of the root crown, not the length of the container itself (see the Planting a Contain-erized Tree section for instructions on identifying the root crown). For a tree in a size #5 container (often referred to as a 5-gallon container), this is very often the same length as that of the shovel blade. When planting bareroot trees, dig to the depth of the tree's root system.

Avoid loosening any soil at the bottom of the planting hole; fluffed-up soil at the bottom causes the tree to *settle* when it's watered in after planting. Remember, planting the tree

Above: Consider planting on a slope, up to but not exceeding 45 degrees, in poor drainage areas to prevent roots from becoming waterlogged. Before digging a hole into a slope, create a flat platform on which to do so and dig a hole into the center of that platform.

Below: Some soils are difficult to dig through with a shovel alone. A pickax or digging bar will loosen compacted soils. Always wear protective eye gear when digging in case rocks or debris are propelled out of the hole.

Roots can circle around glazed clay soil walls, so rough up the sides and create notches for roots to take hold.

too deeply will shorten its life. Placing the unplanted tree in the hole periodically to check the depth can be helpful. For larger trees, like boxed specimens or balled and burlapped (B&B), a mechanical auger or backhoe may be needed to dig holes and move the trees—though the most organic method is to plant manually whenever possible.

The planting hole should be *at least* twice as wide as the container or bareroot tree roots, and wider is better. Studies at the University of Arizona showed benefit in digging a planting hole up to five times as wide as the diameter of the container, but no deeper than the length of the root-ball.[27] Most tree root growth proceeds

[27] Tipton, J. L. 1998. "Planting Guidelines: Container Trees & Shrubs." University of Arizona Cooperative Extension, Bulletin #AZ1022.

horizontally, not vertically, so loosen the soil into a wide shallow dish to help establish a healthy root system more quickly. When planting on a slope, first dig a flat shelf into the side of the incline, and then dig the planting hole into the center of the shelf.

Soil

To further help new roots grow out into the surrounding soil, rough up the sides of the planting hole with the shovel, especially in clay soils that become smooth and glazed after contact with the shovel blade. This practice helps prevent tree roots from growing in a circle around the circumference of the planting hole. Circling roots keep trees from anchoring properly, making them susceptible to *windthrow* (blowing over in a gale), and shortens their lives, even when they don't fall over. Cut some notches in the walls of the planting hole in a clay soil to break up the smooth surface.

Place the excavated soil in two piles on opposite sides of the planting hole, close to the edge, to make backfilling easier. Remove large rocks and chop both piles of displaced soil with the shovel blade to break up clods.

Although tree roots can navigate obstacles and grow in rocky soil, if a finer soil is desired in particularly clumpy and rocky conditions, some chicken wire and two helpers will come in handy. First, cut two 5-foot (1.5-m)–long sheets of chicken wire and place them on top of each other. Next, roll the ends up a few inches to hide any sharp edges. Have two volunteers, both wearing thick enough gloves to prevent injury from the edges of the chicken wire, hold the sheets up at waist level. Proceed to shovel soil from the excavated hole on top of the contraption, with the helpers lightly shaking it up and down. Rocks will filter out on top and soil clumps will break through, allowing a fine soil to fall below.

Creating a fine soil with chicken wire is not necessary, unless there are extreme rocky conditions; however, doing so can give a young tree a head start in its new home.

PLANTING A CONTAINERIZED TREE

1. Place the container on its side with the trunk lying over the top of the hole. To remove the tree, grasp the base of the trunk and pull slowly, while also holding the side of the container. If the root-ball does not slide out easily, press down on the sides of the container and roll gently from side to side, being careful not to break branches. Pounding on the sides of the container will also help loosen the contents. For roots growing through the bottom of the container, use pruners or tin snips to cut the container free. When handling the tree outside of its container, put one hand underneath the root-ball to help keep it together.

2. Once the tree has been removed from its container, check the outside of the root-ball for circling roots. *Gently* pull circling roots so they are freed, enabling them to grow outward, away from the base of the tree. Roots that are too thick or tangled to be unraveled by hand may need to be pruned at the last point where they are straight and do not show signs of curvature or circling. Extensive root pruning of containerized trees, even when needed and performed properly, will slow growth of the canopy, sometimes for two to three years.

3. Continue to gently massage and ruffle the soil all the way around the root-ball, to help stimulate root growth. For stressed or weak trees, less root stimulation is better. Transplanting is a tremendous stress for a tree, and a significant amount of its stored energy is required for it to recover, so when in doubt, go easy. Bring the root-ball to the planting hole and place it inside.

Place the tree on its side with the trunk lying over the hole so that when removed from the container it will fall right into place.

A root-bound containerized tree with its soil washed away to show circling roots. If the condition is not corrected prior to planting, the tree may survive for several years without any meaningful growth before eventually dying from girdling roots.

For containerized trees, *gently* massage the root-ball and untangle circling roots so they face outward when planted.

4. The base of a tree's trunk, where the top growth changes and becomes the root growth, is called the *root crown*. It is very important not to bury a tree's root crown. Containerized trees in nurseries have to be watered frequently; a little potting soil washes out of the drainage openings near the bottom of the container with every watering. To correct this loss, soil is added back in, *at the top of the container*, slowly burying the root crown. Find the root crown of containerized trees before planting in order to avoid burying it again in the planting hole.

5. *Gently* remove soil by hand from the top of the root-ball around the base of the trunk until the first good-size *lateral roots* can be seen. On a sapling, these roots may be only as thick as a pencil, but should not be confused with the thin, white, fibrous "feeder" roots. After determining the location of the lateral roots, be sure they will remain at soil level at planting.

Nursery container waste litters landfills, so check your pot for the recycle symbol and wash it first before recycling. If it's not recyclable, please reuse it or donate it to a local gardening nonprofit.

6. Sometimes nurseries don't add any soil to tree containers to deal with erosion after watering, leaving a tree's root system exposed inside the container. Position the root crown correctly, at soil level or just above in this situation as well. Larger trees, boxed specimens, or balled and burlapped (B&B) trees should be planted so the soil level in these "containers" matches the surrounding soil outside the planting hole. Take care not to pile any additional soil on top of these larger root-balls or onto the base of their trunks.

One of the most critical elements to planting a tree is to do so at the correct depth. Carefully identify the tree's lateral roots (left) and root crown (middle), and then backfill the hole so the first lateral roots are at the same level as the surrounding soil (right). This is applicable to both containerized and bareroot trees.

PLANTING A BAREROOT TREE

1. Before planting bareroot trees, remove dead roots with pruners. Dead roots are typically blackened, dry, and brittle while healthy roots are white or yellow and flexible. If unsure, err on the side of caution and do not remove any portion of the root.

2. Soak the roots in water for about two hours just prior to planting. Do not allow roots to remain in the direct sunlight and open air for long; they can be damaged in as little as fifteen minutes. If the planting process is interrupted, remember to *heel in* bareroot trees again.

3. On bareroot trees, the root crown is much easier to identify because the roots are completely exposed. Position the root crown relative to the surrounding soil level in the same way as for containerized trees—at soil level or 1 to 2 inches (2.5 to 5.1 cm) above. Planting root crowns a little high with bareroot trees helps ensure planting at the right depth, even with some soil settling. To accomplish this, build a small mound at the bottom of the planting hole with backfill soil. Tamp it very firmly to make a pedestal. Spread the roots of the bareroot tree over this pedestal. For reference, the surrounding soil level should *always* be several inches below the graft union.

CHECKING DEPTH AND ORIENTATION

Place the shovel handle flat across the open top of the planting hole. The bottom edge of the shovel's handle, which is where the hole will be backfilled to, should be just above the lateral root system and should meet the root crown. If it doesn't, make as many adjustments as needed to get this just right. Otherwise, burying the root crown kills trees, sometimes quickly, sometimes not for years.

Trees planted too deeply are more susceptible to disease and rotting from water pooling around the trunk, and from insufficient oxygen to the roots. Trees that do not die right away are still more vulnerable to disease because of the stress of growing in an oxygen-poor soil. Burying the root crown kills trees years later because significant root defects develop, or get worse. Roots that grow up, toward the soil's surface for more oxygen, often become stem-girdling roots: roots that closely circle the trunk. With time, the trunk's girth increases, and the root's does too, gradually compressing the trunk. The end result? Stunted trees, with sparse, poorly colored foliage, can linger for years, but they can be snapped in a moment at their weakened bases in a storm.

Spread bareroot tree roots out over a shallow mound to provide support before backfilling to the proper depth. Bareroot trees should always be stored out of the sun with their roots covered in moist soil or sawdust.

If the depth is adjusted by placing soil at the bottom of the planting hole, be sure to tamp it down as firmly as possible. Stomping on the bottom of the planting hole works well. Make sure the tree is standing up straight in the planting hole before backfilling. Walk all the way around the tree to check; the tree may look straight from one angle but crooked from another. Remove all nursery stakes completely and loosen or remove any remaining tags to prevent them from cutting into the tree as it grows.

When fruitwood is grafted to rootstock, the wounds on the trunk heal but remain vulnerable. This is called the *graft union*; protect it from damage by facing it away from the sun—to the north in the northern hemisphere and to the south in the southern hemisphere.

While the root crowns of trees must never be buried, sometimes raising or lowering the entire root-ball in relation to the surrounding soil is beneficial. In poorly draining soils, plant the root-ball 1 or 2 inches (2.5 to 5.1 cm) high. In climates where irrigation and rainfall are scarce, the root-ball and planting hole may be placed a few inches lower than the surrounding soil to help create a basin to capture and retain water.

Below left: Under extreme conditions only, where water is scarce, trees may be planted in shallow pits in order to attract and store water reserves.

Below: A tool's handle or a stick makes for a great measuring device to ensure that the tree is being planted at the correct depth, just above the lateral roots at the root crown. When planting on a slope, always be sure to lay the tool perpendicular to the incline of the slope.

BACKFILL

Use the excavated, sifted soil piled beside the planting hole to fill in around the roots of the newly planted tree. *Do not add anything to this soil,* called the *backfill:* no compost, fertilizer, manure, gravel, sand—*nothing.* Water does not drain from one soil layer into an abruptly different type of soil layer until the first is completely saturated. As a result, amending the backfill creates a container in the ground with no drainage hole—a place for a new tree to become waterlogged and die.

Even if an amended backfill drains well enough into the surrounding native soil, it creates another problem. When tree roots reach the edge of an amended backfill, they circle this perimeter, rather than penetrate the native soil. By amending the backfill, a container is essentially created in the ground that will eventually lead to a root-bound tree. Tree roots are different than those of other annual plants, which are often placed in amended backfill because they are shallow. Tree roots must venture out into the native soil to become anchored and thrive, and amended backfill is detrimental to this process.

Do not apply fertilizers at planting time. Avoid fertilizing a newly planted tree for ninety days to one year after planting. Trees expend stored energy to take up and use fertilizer; fertilization is a stress for a tree. Transplanting is a big stressor for trees, and fertilizing at planting time just adds to the burden.

Once the planting hole is backfilled about halfway, stop and use the shovel blade in a slicing motion, straight up and down through the backfill, all the way around the planting hole. *Be careful not to slice into the root-ball.* This will break up any last clods and eliminate air pockets. Tamp the area by hand and dampen the backfill to encourage soil to settle. Fill in the rest of the planting hole with the remaining backfill and repeat the slicing/hand tamping procedure. Avoid stomping on the backfill or the root-ball. Dampen the backfill again to encourage soil to settle and replace any depressions that form with additional soil.

Above: Check the tree for straightness from different angles. If the area is prone to heavy winds from a particular direction, *slightly* tilt the tree toward that direction.

Below: Tree roots grow laterally and should be encouraged to grow into the native soil. Amending the soil impedes roots from doing so and is universally advised against by authorities such as the International Society of Arboriculture. A bow rake makes for an excellent tool to pull soil into the hole when backfilling. Often, it is faster and easier to fill a hole this way than with a shovel.

BERMS

Use leftover backfill with discarded clods and rocks to make a *berm* to form a water well around the newly planted tree. This will help capture and contain water, allowing it to percolate into the root-ball and surrounding soil. If there is no backfill leftover, borrow some from nearby. The berm should be about 6 inches (15.2 cm) high and positioned just outside the tree's *dripline*. The dripline is the edge of the canopy, where the branches end. For saplings with short, few, or no branches, put the berm 6 to 12 inches (15.2 to 30.5 cm) outside the edge of the root-ball. Tamp the berm firmly (hands and feet are permitted), so it stays together when wet.

MULCH

Mulches are natural materials applied around the base of a tree to help retain water by slowing evaporation from the soil's surface, keep the soil cooler in the summer and warmer in the winter, and suppress weed growth, which decreases competition for water and soil nutrients. Additionally, vegetation-based mulches add nutrients to soil as they slowly decompose. Typical mulching materials include wood chips, shredded bark, straw, hay, leaf litter, and ground rock. Decomposed granite is commonly used as a mineral mulch in very arid climates and populated areas in fire-prone lands.

Use a vegetation-based mulch with a coarse texture in windy climates; they are less likely to blow away and end up in a neighbor's orchard instead. Wood chips provide strong water retention qualities and are long-lasting, unlike other materials that decompose quickly and require frequent reapplications. Mulching the surface of a planted area benefits trees, without altering water drainage through soil layers, or stressing trees like chemical fertilizers. Mulch also provides a finished look to a new planting, which helps while waiting for skinny, little trees to grow into something more pleasing to the eye.

Left: Stones removed from the planting hole or other materials such as upside-down sod clumps can be used to create a pretty border on the outside of a berm for additional support—not to mention a fun family project for all ages.

Below: Place the berm 6 to 12 inches (15.2 to 30.5 cm) beyond the tree's dripline to encourage roots to venture out by seeking moisture in adjacent soils. Berms should be periodically moved outward as the tree's dripline expands.

To Mulch a Newly Planted Tree

1. Apply a thin layer of compost to the area inside the water well, and a 4-to-6-inch (10.2 to 15.2 cm) layer of mulch on top of that. Do not pile compost or mulch against the tree's trunk, which can keep it constantly moist. This promotes decay and infestations. Keep a few inches at the trunk completely clear. If the circle cleared of grass and weeds extends beyond the water well, cover it with 6 inches (15.2 cm) of mulch to help keep weeds from returning.

2. Water the newly planted trees immediately after mulching, especially if using lightweight mulches to anchor them in place. Fill up the water wells completely and let them drain; repeat two to five times. For at least the first month after planting, water the trees in this way twice a week (three times a week if conditions are hot and dry). After that, begin to alter irrigation to a more infrequent regime. See chapter 5, Irrigation and Fertilization, for more details.

Above: Mulching is one of the most enjoyable steps in the planting process. Get creative with your mulch application and make it look pretty! Doughnut-shaped mulch jobs are particularly satisfying to create.

Below: Use recycled mulching materials when possible. Dried organic matter from the yard works well. Many local government entities and tree chipping services provide donated or low-cost mulch to local residents. These options are much better for the environment than purchasing heavily packaged mulch that has been shipped vast distances. The wood chips, compost, and grass clippings pictured here are all local and recycled.

STAKING

A newly planted tree does not have roots anchored in the soil—yet. In the meantime, it may need to be staked; however, staking a tree incorrectly, or for too long, can do more harm than good. Tree stakes can be removed from ninety days to one year after planting. They are not a permanent fixture and must be removed at some point. If a newly planted tree stands up after planting and is not exposed to strong, prevailing winds, or at risk of vandalism, *do not stake it.*

For trees that do not stand on their own, carefully stake them just prior to mulching. FTPF prefers recycled wooden posts that are at least 4 feet (1.2 m) in length and 2 inches (5.1 cm) squared in diameter—two per tree. If recycled materials are not available, most home improvement stores sell 8-foot (2.4 m) two-by-twos for a reasonable price. Use a handsaw or circular saw to cut the 8-foot (2.4 m) post in half, making a diagonal cut to create pointed ends.

1. Place the first post 3 to 6 inches (7.6 to 15.2 cm) *outside* of the root-ball area and use a post pounder to drive it until secure. Drive the other post on the opposite side of the tree. The line created by the posts should be perpendicular to the direction of the prevailing wind.

2. To attach the tree to the stakes, use a wide, flexible tie material with good prehensile strength, such as the staking tapes sold at many nurseries—or better yet, look for recycled materials around your home, as long as they won't damage or cut into the trunk (e.g., never use wire or materials with sharp edges). Some use cut sections of hose to create a soft wrap around the trunk. Wrap the tie in a figure-eight pattern around the post and the lowest point on the tree trunk that will hold it upright (usually 12 to 18 inches [30.5 to 45.7 cm] from the base of a 4-to-7-foot [1.2 to 2.1-m]–tall sapling). Fasten the ends of the tie with a staple gun to the

Staking a Tree (Side View)

Tie the trunk at the lowest point that creates stability.

Drive the stakes just outside the root-ball area.

Stake the tree only if necessary, always use at least two posts, and allow a natural degree of movement by tying the trunk to each post with a figure-eight pattern (see top view diagram). Remove stakes as soon as the tree can stand on its own.

wooden post or hammer a nail into the post to create a hook to tie around. Fasten the second tie to the opposite post about 12 inches (30.5 cm) higher than the first.

3. Be careful not to stake the tree too tightly. Ties that are too snug can damage bark through friction and abrasion; tree trunks immobilized by stake ties fail to develop enough strength to stand on their own. The tree needs to be moved by the wind a little inside the stake ties. Test this by wiggling the trunk to make sure it has a natural degree of movement in all directions.

4. If vandalism is a problem, tree stakes can provide something of a deterrent, or an alternate target. A triangular pattern using three stakes may be more effective in achieving this. Triangular staking also helps in areas with frequent lawn maintenance to protect tree trunks from lawn mower and weed-whip damage.

Staking a Tree (Top View)

Wrap ties in a figure-eight pattern, not too tightly, allowing for a natural degree of movement.

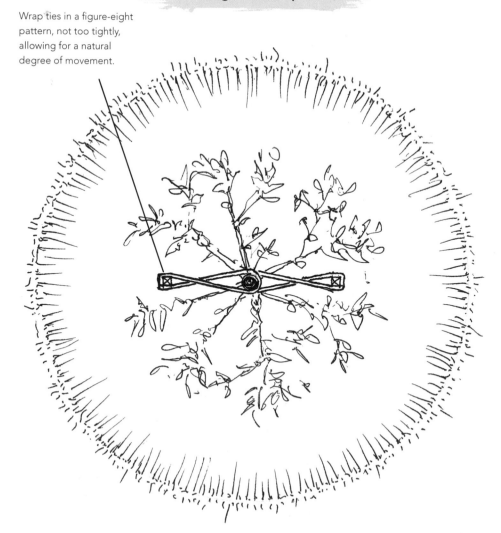

PLANTING PROCEDURE CHECKLIST

✓ Time the planting and obtain trees

✓ Spot trees in the planting layout

✓ Gather tools and materials

✓ Remove grasses and vegetation in a circular pattern around each tree placement

✓ Dig the planting hole exactly as deep as the root-ball and at least twice as wide

✓ Place the tree in the planting hole and adjust to prevent burying the root crown

✓ Gently untangle circling roots and massage the root-ball

✓ Face the tree's graft union away from the sun

✓ Straighten the tree

✓ Backfill the hole *without* amending the backfill

✓ Create a 6-inch (15.2-cm)–tall berm just beyond the tree's dripline

✓ Add a thin layer of compost inside the water well.

✓ Add a 3-to-4-inch (7.6 to 10.2 cm) layer of mulch in the water well, keeping a 2-inch (5.1 cm) radius around the trunk clear

✓ Only when necessary, stake trees with two posts forming a line perpendicular to the prevailing wind

✓ Water the newly planted trees by filling the water wells two to five times

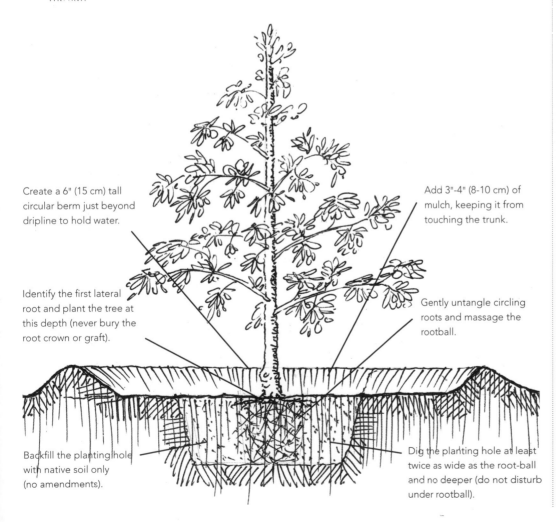

Create a 6" (15 cm) tall circular berm just beyond dripline to hold water.

Identify the first lateral root and plant the tree at this depth (never bury the root crown or graft).

Backfill the planting hole with native soil only (no amendments).

Add 3"-4" (8-10 cm) of mulch, keeping it from touching the trunk.

Gently untangle circling roots and massage the rootball.

Dig the planting hole at least twice as wide as the root-ball and no deeper (do not disturb under rootball).

Properly planted fruit trees can live for decades. Enjoy!

chapter five

IRRIGATION AND FERTILIZATION

I rrigation and fertilization go hand in hand, with fertilizers often included in watering schedules and systems. They are also both elements *added* to an orchard, so they are discussed together in this chapter.

IRRIGATION

Water is sticky. It clings to itself and to the objects it falls onto or into, including soil. Water doesn't ever sit still; it is always moving. Even a stagnant puddle evaporates water from its surface, while more seeps into the ground below. Water takes three forms: solid (ice), liquid, and vapor. Trees depend on water and its properties for their entire lives. Tree leaves let water vapor escape through pores in their undersides, called *stomata*. This water loss, *transpiration*, keeps trees cool. Every water molecule lost through the stomata must be, and is, instantly replaced with a new one. Because water sticks to itself, a property called *cohesion*, a chain of water molecules lines up behind all the stomata, and throughout the tree. Trees and plants are composed of about 85 percent water. Roots expend energy to take in water from the soil, but from then on, trees take advantage of cohesion to form a column of water from their roots to their highest leaf tip. When a water molecule returns to the atmosphere, it pulls the next one into place behind it, which pulls another behind it, and so on, all the way down to the ends of the roots. As a result, trees do not use their own energy to accomplish this. The amount of water transpired into the air can be enormous; on a hot summer day, a large mature tree may release more than 100 gallons (379 L) of water back into the atmosphere.

Inside the Tree

Water inside trees carries dissolved minerals absorbed by roots. These nutrients are distributed through the tree by cohesion as well. Plant tissues holding sufficient water are turgid; they are swollen enough to keep their cell walls upright. *Turgidity* helps trees stand, branches and twigs extend, and leaves remain outstretched to gather the sun's rays. Wilting plants and trees display a loss of turgidity. Water provides for both stiffness and flexibility in trees. Living wood, holding enough water within, bends further before breaking. Water also offers

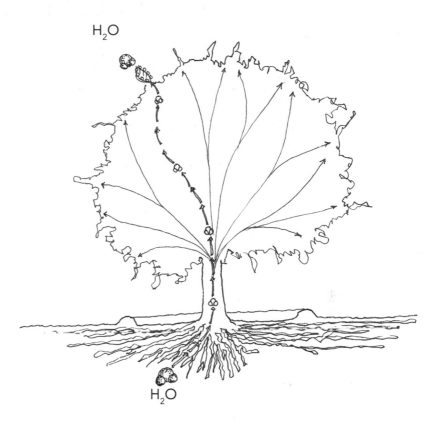

some protection against the cold. Under the same weather conditions, well-watered trees suffer less frost damage than drought-stressed ones. Roots coax water from the soil using osmosis. Water inside roots is saltier than that in the soil, and so, water flows into roots to balance the difference. (Should the reverse situation arise, water can move out of roots, back into the soil, which is disastrous for plants.)

Drought stress

All of these processes move along swimmingly, so long as the water supply in the soil remains adequate. Drought stress begins when water available to roots is less than enough to meet the tree's needs. A first symptom of drough stress is a certain off-color look to leaves, a kind of dull, blue-gray unhappiness. Leaves wilt next. If water needs continue to go unmet, leaves will dry and drop off. If the situation doesn't improve, gradual dieback of wood progresses from twigs to branches to the

The cohesion-tension principle explains how water moves from the roots to the tip of a tree's leaves, against gravity, without expending energy.

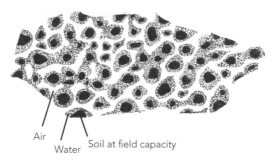

Air
Water
Soil at field capacity

Field Capacity

Farmers and soil scientists use the term *field capacity (FC)* to denote the maximum amount of water a soil can hold in the root zone, against the force of gravity. A soil at FC is not saturated; pore space is filled with roughly half air, half water. Field capacity is greater for clayey soils than for sandy soils. Clay loams hold the most plant available water at field capacity.

Moisture sensors, devices designed to read soil moisture levels, have become more accurate, easier to maintain and widely available in recent years. A hands-on "feel test" can be just as helpful in gauging soil moisture levels. With a spade, dig down 6 to 8 inches (15.2 to 20.3 cm) and take up a handful of soil. Squeeze it. For any of the soil texture types, a ball of soil at FC, squeezed, will not release free water, but will leave a sheen of moisture on the palm. It's time to irrigate when soil in the root zone is at 50 percent of field capacity. At this soil moisture level, sandy soils feel dry and will not form a ball at all. A clay loam will form a crumbly one.

trunk. Roots are dying back, too. Decline in fruit quantity and quality starts *before* the first visible symptom of drought stress. Fruit trees need consistent soil moisture from bloom to harvest. Beginning to water fruit trees two to three weeks before the first blooms open may be necessary to build up moisture in the soil following dry winters. Preventing drought stress saves trees energy, improves their health, and results in larger, juicer, tastier fruits, and more of them. When rainfall is inconsistent or insufficient, irrigate fruit trees.

Think of soil as a reservoir. Learn about the orchard soil's water-holding capacity. By the time the trees show drought stress, water deficiency is already significant. Don't wait for the trees to say they need water. Know they do ahead of time; know the soil. Soil texture, sandy to clayey, discussed earlier, dictates the infiltration rate, and how far horizontally water will spread as it soaks in. Soil texture also influences the amount of water available to plant roots. Water's other sticky property, *adhesion*, causes water molecules to cloak soil particles. Clay particles form the tightest bond with water molecules, sand particles the loosest. Water molecules closest to soil particles are held more tightly than those farther away in the soil's pore spaces. Cohesion and adhesion routinely defy gravity, but water not held by either is pulled down through the soil, past the root zone, until it joins the groundwater. This lost water, called *gravitational water*, and water held by adhesion is unavailable to plant roots. Water out in the soil's pore spaces is the available water.

Above: Soil structure largely determines how much water is available to trees after watering. Field capacity refers to the state where the most amount of water is available within a soil's pores for tree roots—roughly when the space between soil particles is half air, half water, as depicted here.

Right: Dig down 6 to 8 inches (15.2 to 20.3 cm) to test if the soil is moist or dry to determine how frequently to water.

Water Loss

Soils receive water from either precipitation (rain or snow) or from irrigation, which is water applied by anything from a handheld hose to an automatic sprinkler system. Soils lose water through evaporation from their surfaces, transpiration of plants and trees, runoff, and *leaching* (gravity pulling water down past the root zone). Soils, from sandy loams through clays, hold an average of 2 inches (5.1 cm) of available water per foot (30.5 cm) of rooting depth. For example, a soil 3 feet (0.9 m) deep holds about 6 inches (15.2 cm) of water for tree roots. The time it takes for trees to draw that available water down halfway, to 3 inches (7.6 cm) in this example, should be the interval between irrigations. Soil water losses from evaporation and transpiration are combined and called *evapotranspiration*, or *ET*. ET rates reveal how much water is lost from soil reservoirs over a time interval. Regional governments collect data for ET rates, daily or weekly, and publish results along with other weather information.

WATER NEEDS

For fruit trees, how big they are, and how hot it is outside, determines the amount of water the trees withdraw from the soil. Water needs vary somewhat between different fruit tree types, but canopy size is really the biggest factor. Canopy size measured in square feet, combined with weather data, provides estimates of daily per tree water use. For example, a tree with a 100-square-foot (30.5 m²) canopy (10 feet high x 10 feet wide, or 3 m high x 3 m wide) on a hot mid-summer day, on California's central coast will use about 16 gallons (61 L) of water.[28] Fruit tree water use estimates are also available from local Agricultural Extensions or Master Gardener's programs.

[28] Pittenger, D.R. 2004. Publication #3382, University of California, Agriculture and Natural Resources.

Additional irrigation is also sometimes needed to flush accumulated salts from the root zone, to keep them in a solution less salty than inside the roots. Annual precipitation may be enough to accomplish this; however, when it is not, such as in arid climates, additional irrigation is required.

Knowing your soil and knowing your trees comes with time, experience, and a watchful eye. At first, a great deal of attention must be paid, but after a few growing seasons, knowing when and how much to irrigate gets a little easier to figure out. To start off, just remember that newly planted trees need more frequent watering, with smaller amounts, than established trees. Home orchards can be irrigated by any one of three different methods: flood, sprinkler, or micro-irrigation.

FLOOD IRRIGATION

Flood irrigation means filling up a basin or trough surrounding fruit trees, once or a number of times, until the correct amount of water is applied. Intervals between irrigations depend on the soil's water holding capacity, and the rate of use by the trees. Filling up the water wells for newly planted trees, as described in chapter 4, Planting, is flood irrigation. This method is commonly used for backyard and commercial orchards alike. Basins for individual trees should be about 12 inches (30.5 cm) outside the dripline. Berms surrounding a row of trees should also sit outside the dripline, along the sides, and at each end. Berm walls should be tall enough to accommodate both water and mulch, roughly, the sum of each. So, to put down 3 inches (7.6 cm) of water and 3 inches (7.6 cm) of mulch, berms should be 6 to 8 inches (15.2 to 20.3 cm) high. Another berm may be built inside the basin, around the trunk of each tree. These inside berms, positioned 8 to 12 inches (20.3 to 30.5 cm) away from the trunk of an established tree, closer for younger trees, keep water away from the trunk and the root crown. Do not mulch between the tree and the inside berm. Keeping the trunk and the root crown dry prevents disease.

Flood irrigation schedules need to be deep and infrequent—wetting the entire root zone and letting it dry to 50 percent of field capacity before the next watering. Fruit trees can be flood irrigated by hand with a hose or with an irrigation system. A conventional irrigation system with bubblers rather than spray heads can be used to fill basins. In wet-season climates, break out sections of berm walls to let excess water drain away when the rains come.

Flood Irrigation Pros

✓ Easy to install

✓ Low cost to build

✓ Longer intervals between watering

✓ Waters the entire root zone

✓ Useful for leaching salts from root zone

✓ Shortest irrigation system run time

Flood Irrigation Cons

✓ Easy to overwater and waste water

✓ More area for weed growth

✓ Watered area must be flat

✓ Not good for very sandy or very clayey soils

✓ Easy to leach nutrients and fertilizers past root zone

SPRINKLER IRRIGATION

Sprinkler irrigation systems can also be used to water home orchards. The entire root zone gets wet, just like it does with flood irrigation, but sprinklers have to run longer to put down the same amount of water. The *precipitation rate* measures how quickly a depth of water is dispersed (for example, inches per hour). The precipitation rate varies widely among the different types of sprinklers available, but for each sprinkler head on a single system, it should match. Matched precipitation rates help to ensure that water is applied evenly throughout the area covered by the sprinkler system. This means that the soil will be watered to roughly the same depth throughout the orchard after irrigation.

It's important to provide consistent moisture for each tree, and to be good environmental stewards by being as efficient with water as possible. Sprinkler systems lose more to evaporation because water is thrown into the air. Sprinkler precipitation rates should not exceed the soil's infiltration rate—don't put down water faster than the soil can take it in.

Flood irrigation can be as simple as building a berm and filling it manually with a hose or with the help of Mother Nature through rainwater harvesting.

Sprinkler head types abound: spray heads, stream rotors, variable arc rotors, and impact heads. A range of options is available within each type for spray pattern, throw distance, and precipitation rates. There's a sprinkler designed for every soil under the sun. The lower the precipitation rate, the longer the system needs to run to thoroughly wet the root zone. Putting down water more slowly can be a good strategy for soils with slow infiltration rates or sloping terrain.

Sprinkler systems are best for orchards with multiple trees planted together. For trees separated by some distance, choose flood or micro-irrigation methods. Use sprinkler systems to replenish the soil reservoir, applying water at intervals corresponding to the time it takes to reach 50 percent of field capacity. Use the feel test, just like for flood irrigation, to find out how many days go by before the soil dries out to that point. Remember, drought stress affects fruit quality before signs are visible on the tree. Check the soil for moisture levels; don't wait for the tree's signals.

Sprinkler Irrigation Pros

✓ Disperses water more slowly than flooding

✓ Wets the entire root zone

✓ Better choice for sites that are not flat

✓ Can be used for very sandy or clayey soils

Sprinkler Irrigation Cons

✓ Harder to keep trees and fruit dry

✓ More expensive to install than flood systems

✓ Needs more maintenance and adjustments

✓ Water lost to overspray and evaporation

✓ More area for weed growth

Sprinkler systems (pictured here) and drip irrigation may be automated, for example, through the use of a timer, allowing the home orchardist to be away from the site yet still provide irrigation for trees.

MICRO-IRRIGATION

Micro-irrigation, also called drip irrigation, is the most water-efficient irrigation technology around. Invented in Israel, it was designed to grow plants and trees in arid lands. Today, micro-irrigation systems are used all over the world, for agriculture and horticulture. Conventional sprinkler systems operate at water pressures above 50 psi (pounds per square inch), or 345 kPa, and disperse water at rates measured in gallons per minute. Micro-irrigation systems operate from 10 to 30 psi (69 to 207 kPa), at the emitter, and their flow rates are measured in gallons *per hour*. This slow release of water to the root zone, right at the soil's surface, dramatically reduces waste from evaporation and runoff. Some systems are designed to be buried just under the surface. Water applications are concentrated around each tree, and only a portion of the root zone gets wet, not the whole thing. Root growth is dense in these moist spots. How far water will spread from the emitter depends on the soil type. Wetting patterns are more narrow and vertical in sandy soils, more broad and shallow in clays.

Contrary to myth, roots do not grow in search of water. Roots only grow where soil is moist already; they cannot grow through dry soil. Trees sustained by micro-irrigation systems grow their roots in the parts of the soil kept wet by the emitters. Keeping just 20 to 50 percent of the root zone consistently irrigated is enough to maintain a fruit tree. Spacing emitters throughout and around the dripline is critical to ensure that the tree can provide itself adequate anchorage. Do not abandon trees to a short difficult life by leaving just one or two emitters, right next to the trunk, for years after planting. Adding and adjusting the positions of emitters as trees grow to maturity is essential to help them thrive on a micro-irrigation system. For sandy soils, space emitters 12 inches (30.5 cm) apart within and just beyond the dripline (but not right against the trunk), 18 inches (45.7 cm) for loams, 24 inches (61 cm) for clays.[29]

Micro-irrigation is efficient but not easy. These systems have more components that require diligent maintenance to keep them operating correctly. Some are expensive to install, while others, such as above-ground drip lines, are relatively inexpensive, with additional savings and peace of mind achieved through efficient water use. Emitters have evolved from the tiny plastic "bug" at the end of a black flexible tube to include in-line emitters, microspray heads, and low-volume bubblers. The maintenance issues remain the same for each type, however; without water filtration and regular inspection, drip emitters become clogged. Debris, dirt, or insects can plug up tiny orifices from inside or out. For emitters other than microspray heads, a clogged emitter cannot be spotted just by turning the system on and taking a casual glance at the orchard. Sometimes, a dead tree is the first visible sign of clogged emitters. Aside from emitter choice, the structural components of a micro-irrigation system are similar: connection to the water source, control valve (on-off switch), mainline flexible pipe, and lateral line tubing.

Approach scheduling micro-irrigation differently than flood or sprinkler systems. Don't think of the soil as a reservoir when using micro-irrigation. Instead, maintain constant moisture in the root zone, sufficient to replace daily evapotranspiration. This doesn't mean running the system every day, but it might mean running it every other day during the heat of summer. Emitters release water in gallons per hour, so putting down inches of water can take hours, not minutes.

See the chart on page 88 for sample irrigation schedules for each of the irrigation types.

[29] Hill, R. W. 2008. Ag/Small Acreage/2008-01pr. Utah State University Cooperative Extension.

Micro-irrigation Pros

✓ Disperses water more slowly than flooding

✓ Efficient use of water

✓ Fits in small, odd-shaped, or sloped sites

✓ Saves money with lower water costs

✓ Liquid fertilizers can be run through the system

✓ System operation can be automatic with an installed timer

✓ Less area for weed growth

✓ Trees and fruit stay dry

✓ Lightweight parts make installation easy

✓ Entire system can be above ground

Micro-irrigation Cons

✓ Increased maintenance

✓ Emitters can clog

✓ Many components to a complex system

✓ Soil salts collect around wetted area edges

✓ Long run times

Drip irrigation parts are readily available at gardening and online outlets and are easy to install. Mainline tubing is hooked to a spigot and rolled out in the orchard (the other end is eventually closed with an end cap). **(1)** The tube may be split or placed on valves that direct water flow to different parts of the orchard, especially if water pressure isn't high enough to run every bubbler at once. **(2)** Thinner, microlines are attached to the mainline through hole-punched openings and extended to each tree with a bubbler at the end of each. **(3)** The bubbler can be adjusted to control water flow, and **(4)** moved with the dripline as the tree grows.

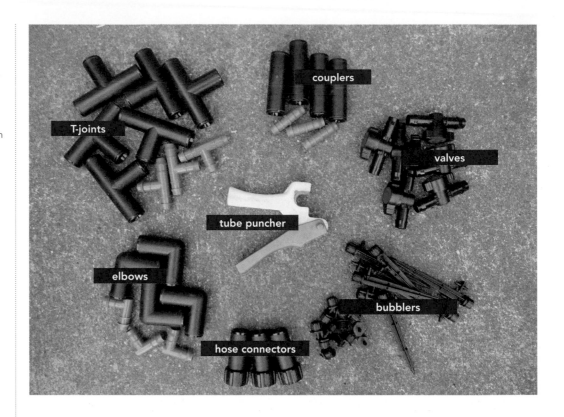

T-joints

couplers

valves

tube puncher

elbows

bubblers

hose connectors

WATERING SCHEDULE GUIDELINES

The technology of irrigation systems is not the sole answer to water conservation, efficient use of water, or being "water-wise." Knowing how much water fruit trees need, when they need it, and how much water the soil will hold is. Some general rules of thumb for newly planted trees until the specific water requirements of the orchard are determined are as follows.

✓ Unless planting in areas with extremely high rainfall or with native tree species adapted to grow in the wild, irrigation is required for fruit trees to thrive. Even in areas of high rainfall, a water source is needed for times of drought or extreme heat.

Dig down 6 to 8 inches (15.2 to 20.3 cm) and take up a handful of soil. Squeeze it. If the soil feels dry or crumbly, or both, it is time to water. If the soil is moist, then the tree is receiving adequate water.

✓ Irrigate trees deeply rather than shallowly and more frequently. Picture the root zone in the ground and water the soil to the bottom of the root-ball.

✓ In general, during the early growing season, water newly planted trees deeply at least once a week. During warmer parts of the growing season, at least twice a week. In winter months, keep soils around newly planted trees *slightly* moistened. Significant rain or snowfall may be counted as a watering, and trees may not need additional irrigation during wet seasons.

✓ Trees in heavy clay soils may be watered less frequently, and those in very sandy soils more frequently.

✓ Keep your soils moist but not saturated. Water-logged soils will displace oxygen that roots need for survival. Overwatering often results in symptoms similar to not watering enough. Standing pools of water in the basin for 24 hours or more are a sign of poor drainage or overwatering, or both.

✓ Watch fruit trees for signs of drought stress, which may appear as loss of leaf sheen, wilting, and leaf drop.

✓ As the tree matures, water applications should be expanded with the dripline and just beyond.

WATERING SCHEDULE COMPARISONS

The following table shows a sample irrigation schedule for different emitters and sprinklers, for the same tree and the same weather on one day to give a sense of water needs. Specifically, this example assumes a semidwarf, temperate zone fruit tree with a 100-square-foot (30.5 m) canopy, in mid-summer, with an ET rate of 16

gallons (61 L). The same daily ET is used to calculate the one- and two-week schedules even though these fluctuate and are not constant in reality. Flow rates for the sprinklers and emitters listed are both approximate and typical for their type. *N/A* means that schedule is not recommended for that system type. Long run times can be broken into fractions spaced through the week (e.g., 8 hours into half for 4 hours, 3 days apart). Always strive, however, for a deep, infrequent watering regime.

When using the soil as a reservoir, attempt to wet the root zone to a depth of 3 feet (0.9 m) for mature fruit trees. When long run times exceed the soil's infiltration rate, use multiple cycles (e.g., 3 cycles, 1 hour each, 2 hours apart, on the same day, to achieve a 3-hour run

Certain trees require chilly conditions in order to set fruit. Heavy snow may be considered a watering— not to mention a beautiful wintry backdrop.

time). For flood irrigation by hand: 1 inch (2.5 cm) of water applied to 1 square foot (30.5 cm²) of soil surface equals 0.62 gallons (2.3 L) of water. For sandy soils, 1 inch (2.5 cm) of water penetrates about 12 inches (30.5 cm) deep (but they dry out faster), 8 inches (20.3 cm) deep for loams, and 4 to 5 inches (10.2 to 12.7 cm) for clays.

Irrigation schedule comparison chart for a semidwarf, temperate zone fruit tree with a 100-square-foot (30.5 m) canopy, in mid-summer, with an ET rate of 16 gallons (61 L)

Irrigation Type	Flow Rate	Time to Replace ET	1-Day Run Time	1-Week Run Time	2-Week Run Time
Micro-irrigation: 4 emitters per tree (1 gallon per hour per emitter)	4 gph (15 Lph)	4 hours	4 hours	28 hours	N/A
Micro-irrigation: Microspray	10 gph (38 Lph)	1 hour, 36 minutes	1 hour, 36 minutes	11 hours, 12 minutes	N/A
Sprinkler: Stream rotor	1.25 gpm (4.7 Lpm)	13 minutes	N/A	91 minutes	3 hours
Sprinkler: Spray head	1.85 gpm (7 Lpm)	9 minutes	N/A	63 minutes	2 hours, 6 minutes
Flood Irrigation	2 gpm (7.6 Lpm)	8 minutes	N/A	56 minutes	1 hour, 52 minutes

Rainwater Harvesting

Water harvesting is the art of capturing rainwater and saving it for a later use. A rainwater harvesting system, regardless of its degree of complexity, consists of four basic components: collection, storage, distribution, and system maintenance. Collection surfaces can involve any element of a landscape, including rooftops, hardscape, and the soil itself. Storage containers can be used, or water may be retained using the soil directly as a reservoir. If containers are used, they must be covered to inhibit the growth of mosquitoes, and debris should be filtered from the water. Containers can be stored above or below ground. If the soil is used for storage, use of the water harvested for irrigation can be rather immediate. Water that percolates through the soil below the root zone also helps to recharge groundwater.

Gravity is the least expensive distributor of a water harvest. A distribution system that begins with gutters and downspouts, and uses berms, swales, or concave areas to slow and hold water is the simplest. Hardscape, including porous paving, driveways, and walks that are pitched to drain into planter beds, increases the harvest. Perform system maintenance by removing debris from distribution components. Everything from leaf screens at downspouts to mesh filters on a drip irrigation system needs to be properly cleaned to keep harvested rainwater flowing in the intended direction. Maintenance of berms and other water holding features is best performed just before, and just after, the rainy season.

Average annual rainfall and square footage of catchment area are used to calculate the potential rainwater harvest. Roughly, 1 inch (2.5 cm) of rain on 1,000 square feet (305 m²) of rooftop yields about 550 gallons (2,082 L) of water.

The benefits of water harvesting extend beyond water conservation. Rainwater is clean, and besides its low-to-no salt content, it brings atmospheric nitrogen down with it—a fertilizer bonus. Holding rainwater in the soil and storing it in containers means less of it enters storm drains, reducing the burden on those systems and decreasing chances of flooding.

Adoption of a rainwater harvesting culture throughout a region could aid significantly in groundwater recharge and water conservation.

The limitations of rainwater harvesting become most apparent, as do many problems, in urban areas. Smog pollutes rainwater passing through it. Runoff collected from driveways, roads, and parking lots is further polluted by oily residues. Rainfall patterns can be inconsistent, but a minimum of about 8 inches (20.3 cm) total annual liquid precipitation is needed to support a rooftop collection system.

Rainwater harvesting is good for the environment and your orchard. This house gutter is conserving valuable water resources by redirecting rain into the garden.

FERTILIZATION

Air and water supply the carbon, hydrogen, and oxygen trees and plants need; absorbed from the soil, an additional fourteen elements are vital to their growth and survival. The required quantity of each essential nutrient varies from large to miniscule, but each element is equally necessary. A deficiency of any one of them will cause abnormal growth patterns, increased vulnerability to disease, and poor-quality fruit. An excess of some of the essential nutrients can also cause plant health disorders. Trees make sugar for energy through photosynthesis; in the processes of storing and using these sugars, they create proteins and fats, as well. Trees and plants use the essential nutrients absorbed from the soil to build the rest of our food supply.

MACRONUTRIENTS, SECONDARY NUTRIENTS, MICRONUTRIENTS, AND pH

The *macronutrients*, or primary nutrients, trees and plants absorb from the soil are nitrogen, phosphorus, and potassium—called *macro* because of the relatively high amount of the nutrients needed. They are often abbreviated and referred to collectively as *N-P-K* (nitrogen, phosphorus, and potassium, respectively).

Nitrogen, the most commonly deficient nutrient for fruit trees grown in any soil type, promotes green growth. For young trees, meeting nitrogen requirements is important to sustain the rapid shoot growth of the early years. Timing nitrogen applications improves uptake and use of this nutrient. Early spring, before bud break, is a good time for most climates. Symptoms of nitrogen deficiency show up readily in yellowing older leaves, shorter-than-normal shoot growth, and browning leaf edges. It should be noted, however, that overapplication of nitrogen fertilizers is common throughout agriculture and horticulture, and is a significant source of groundwater pollution. Trees exhibit symptoms of excess nitrogen in green leaves that are too dark. Foliage-feeding insects are very attracted to the lush, floppy new growth resulting from an overabundance of nitrogen. Nitrogen excess causes an increase in the occurrence of the disease fire blight in apples and pears.

Phosphorus promotes root growth and fruit and seed maturation. Soils are rarely poor in phosphorus, but this nutrient's availability to tree roots is affected by the soil's pH. Phosphorus deficiency symptoms show up in slow growth rates and stunted trees. The oldest leaves may have a purplish cast, and fruit development may be poor.

Potassium helps to move sugars around inside trees and plants. It opens and closes stomata, and it promotes root growth, disease resistance, and the size and quality of fruits and nuts. Symptoms of potassium deficiency include slow growth rate, leaves with yellow tips and edges, and dead older leaves.

Calcium, *magnesium*, and *sulfur* are called the *secondary nutrients*. Calcium and magnesium can be leached from soil, and calcium deficiencies frequently go undiagnosed. Calcium is a building block for plant cell walls. Plants and trees deficient in this nutrient exhibit small thick leaves, thinning foliage, and fewer fruits. Calcium deficiency causes the disease bitter pit in apples and pears.

Micronutrients are additional elements required in minute quantities. (See the chart on page 96 for a full list.)

pH is a numeric scale used to describe relative acidity or alkalinity. The value 7.0 is neutral. Values lower than 7.0 describe increasingly acidic conditions, and values higher than 7.0 represent increasing alkalinity. The scale is logarithmic: 6.0 is 10 times more acidic than 7.0 and 5.0 is 100 times more. A soil's pH affects the availability of the essential nutrients to be absorbed by roots. Different elements become "locked up" or "fixed" in soils with an acid or alkaline pH. The best range where all of the nutrients are available to be absorbed by roots is 6.5 to 7.5. Soils with pH values below 5.0 are strongly acid, above 8.0, strongly alkaline. Correcting a soil's pH may be more necessary than fertilization to make soil nutrients available to fruit tree roots.

If other trees grow near the orchard site, start by looking at them; check for normal leaf color and shoot growth. Once the fruit trees are planted, watch for the same signs. Know what normal color and shoot growth rates should be for the types of fruit trees planted. Soil test kits, designed for home use, vary in complexity, price, and unfortunately, accuracy. Shop around for more than price and buy from a reputable manufacturer, or send the soil to the lab for professional analysis (many affordable options are available online). Handheld meters to test pH and salt levels are also available. Follow the instructions included with the kit. Test soil in more than one location in the orchard. Know the basics about the orchard's soil: levels of nitrogen, phosphorus, potassium, and pH, at a minimum, before deciding to fertilize.

Soil types and average annual precipitation affect nutrient content and determine fertilization regimes. Sandy soils are generally less fertile than other soil types. Alkaline clays lock up many essential elements. Loams with an *organic* matter content of 4 to 5 percent and a neutral pH are the most fertile soils (organic matter is material derived from the remains of living organisms). No coincidence that they are also well-draining, with good water-holding capacity, good oxygen levels, and support an assortment of microbial life. Soils in arid climates have the lowest percentage of organic matter in their topsoils, often as low as 1 to 2 percent. Soils in temperate-zone climates average 7 to 10 percent organic matter content. Bogs, swamps, and river deltas can have organic matter contents as high as 50 to 75 percent.[30] (It is possible to have too much of a good thing.)

Most soils contain most of the essential elements required for good growth for fruit trees, but no soil has the perfect balance of all of them. The old saying, "Feed the soil to feed the plant," ought to finish with, "to feed ourselves." This section seeks to approach fruit tree fertilization from a soil health building perspective, rather than a spot treatment for specific deficiency strategy.

BUILDING HEALTHY SOIL

Building a healthy soil takes time, years, in fact. If possible, begin before the orchard is planted by incorporating *organic material* into the top 12 inches (30.5 cm) of soil over the *entire* orchard floor. (This is very different from amending the backfill for each planting hole, which is not recommended.) Compost can be spread and tilled in, depending on the orchard's size; a very large amount may be needed. For example: to add compost into the topsoil for a 1,000-square-foot (305 m²) area to 12 inches (30.5 cm) deep at one third of the soil's volume, 333 cubic feet (9424 L), or 12.33 cubic yards (9424 L) is necessary. Adjust this calculation based on the planting site's dimensions by determining the total volume of soil to be amended (width x length x depth) and multiplying this by the desired percentage of compost incorporated. Amending soils at less than 25 percent of the root zone's volume is ineffective.

Another preplanting soil-building option is to grow, mow, and till in a *cover crop*, such as red clover or vetch. *Green manures* may be grown and tilled in repeatedly for one to three years before planting trees. After the orchard is planted out, tilling soil becomes less feasible because of the potential to damage tree roots.

[30] California Fertilizer Association. 1998. *Western Fertilizer Handbook— Second Horticulture Edition*. (Interstate Publishers, Inc.).

Plant green manures, such as these fava beans, and till them into the soil for one to three seasons prior to planting trees for a natural, nutrient-rich substrate without chemicals or store-bought products. Every time a natural solution is used, resources to manufacture, package, and transport products are saved.

Surface applications of compost and mulch to the orchard floor decompose and build the nutrient content and tilth of the soil over time. Whereas fertilizers benefit plant growth by adding essential nutrients to the root zone, and soil amendments improve the physical characteristics of soil (drainage, water-holding capacity, etc.), the addition of organic matter to soils performs both functions; organic matter provides essential nutrients, like fertilizers, and improves the physical characteristics of soils.

The addition of organic matter to the root zone benefits all of the soil types. It helps sandy soils to aggregate (form clods) and develop better water-holding capacity. It helps clays "open up" to form more and larger pore spaces, which improves infiltration rates and drainage. Plant residues added to soil, on the surface or tilled in, decompose through the action of microbes until they become a substance called *humus*.

Humus is organic matter resistant to further decomposition. Microbes making humus release nutrients into the soil in their elemental, or mineralized, form—the only form roots can absorb.

Salt and Nutrient Content of Soil

The difference in fertilizer types, organic or synthetic, lies in the impact they have on the life of the soil. Synthetic fertilizers are salts. Adding salts to soils must be carefully managed to avoid the destruction of soil structure, specifically the obliteration of pore space, and the pollution of groundwater. Animal manures also contain salts. Prepackaged animal waste fertilizers typically come from animals kept in unhealthy conditions on intensive factory farms, and should be avoided. If harvested fresh from well-treated animals, manures should be composted before use as fertilizers. Solid waste from carnivorous animals should not be used as fertilizers in the home orchard.

Plant residues, like compost and green manures, do not have a significant salt content but do not release their nutrients immediately, either. They must be "broken down," decomposed by microflora and fauna living in the root zone, to return to the mineralized form available to roots. It is this journey, not the destination, that builds the health of soil. Slow release of nutrients prevents injury to roots; chemical fertilizer salts applied incorrectly can "burn" roots. Still-decomposing plant residues create a reserve of nutrients held in the soil. The flourishing life of a multitude of different microorganisms benefits trees through increased competition for pathogens and symbiotic relationships with roots. The addition of organic matter, through compost or green manures, gradually lowers the pH of soil. This can take years but may need to be remedied at some point. While soil organic matter is a source of nitrogen, phosphorus, sulfur, and many of the micronutrients, additional supplementation with mineral powders may be needed occasionally—particularly calcium.

The sprouting, growth, flowering, fruiting, and death of plants moves nutrients in a circle out of and back into soil. The rotting of dead plants releases nutrients used by living plants. When crops are removed from the field, their nutrients

FTPF encourages the use of organic, vegan fertilizers only to ensure the most natural balance of nutrients for optimal fruit tree orchard health, and most importantly, to minimize potential detrimental impacts on our environment.

Manually work in compost topically, with a layer of mulch on top, to provide a long-term nutrient boost to soils. Organic seaweed and kelp fertilizers are also effective in providing micronutrients.

What Is Compost Tea?

Compost tea is a liquid fertilizer made by submerging finished compost in water. Constant aeration while brewing facilitates the growth of billions of microorganisms: bacteria, fungi, protozoa, and nematodes. The presence of oxygen throughout the process ensures that the majority of these organisms are beneficial to plants and trees. Microorganisms grown in the absence of oxygen are called anaerobic and are more likely to be pathogens.

Finished compost tea is a highly concentrated fluid mix of microbes and nutrients sprayed onto foliage and the soil surface. Foliar sprays should be applied early in the morning, before the heat of the day. Only small amounts of nutrients can be absorbed through foliage, but they are immediately available to the tree for use. Compost tea is one way to address micronutrient supplementation. The microbes in the brew also provide benefits. The presence of these organisms on leaf surfaces might provide some protection from pests and diseases. The idea is that they survive on a sheen of sugar that coats the leaves, and take up all of the available space—so, there's no room for pathogens to latch on.

Compost teas are used in commercial agriculture, as well as home orchards.

Compost Tea Materials and Recipe

> Two #5 plastic buckets
>
> 1 gallon (3.8 L) finished compost
>
> 1 aquarium pump
>
> 1 gang valve
>
> Several feet of clear flexible aquarium tubing
>
> 4 gallons (15 L) de-chlorinated water
>
> 1 oz (28.3 g) unsulphured, organic molasses

1. Attach tubing from the pump to the gang valve. Measure, cut, and attach three pieces of tubing so that they reach the bottom of a #5 bucket and connect to three ports on the gang valve, which can be hung on the bucket rim. If available, attach small air stones to the three loose ends of the tubing to weigh them down in the bucket.

2. Add the water and run the pump for at least an hour to bubble the water and evaporate the chlorine.

3. Pour in the compost and molasses. Brew the mixture for two to three days.

4. A couple of times a day, use a stick to stir the mix vigorously. Reset the tubing afterward.

Once the tea is brewed, strain it into the empty bucket through layers of cheesecloth or old sheeting. Yield should be 2 to 3 gallons (7.6 to 11.4 L) of compost tea. Put the soaked compost back into the compost pile or spread below trees. Finished compost tea should smell sweet or earthy, not bad. (Do not apply foul-smelling compost tea to foliage.) It can be applied through a sprayer; get a good, clog-free nozzle. Apply all of the finished tea within four hours of straining it to put those living microbes to good use!

go with them. Cropping the soil is the farmer's plight. Tree fruits are composed of sugar and water, for the most part. When they are picked, the trees, and their leaf litter, branch trimmings, etc., stay behind. Cropping of fruit orchard soils is minimal and very slow. Chip and return all disease-free leaf litter and pruned branches to the orchard floor with mulch to maintain nutrients in the root zone.

Fertilization needs are greatest for young fruit trees and taper off to a stable level for mature trees. Exact pounds of fertilizer, per tree, per year will not be listed here—that varies with fruit tree type, soil composition, and climate. Check with Agricultural Extension or Natural Resource Conservation offices for information about local soils. Soil maps may be available.

Essential Nutrients Needed for Healthy Orchards

Macronutrients	Secondary Nutrients	Micronutrients
Carbon	Calcium	Zinc
Hydrogen	Magnesium	Iron
Oxygen	Sulfur	Manganese
Nitrogen		Copper
Phosphorus		Boron
Potassium		Molybdenum
		Chlorine
		Nickel

Organic Options for Citrus Trees

Citrus trees have a reputation for being "heavy feeders." Fertilizers are not plant food; plants and trees make their own food. Citrus are, however, prone to multiple nutrient deficiencies, and often fertilized with synthetic fertilizers. The recipe below is one option in pursuing an organic fertilization regime for citrus. Please note that application rates are for mature trees and need to be buried in the soil to a depth of 12 inches (30.5 cm). Please also note that cottonseed meal frequently contains significant pesticide residues and most commercially grown soybeans are genetically modified, so look for organic, non-GMO options.

> 4 parts cottonseed meal or soybean meal (for nitrogen, phosphorus, and potassium)
>
> 1 part dolomitic limestone, powdered (for calcium and magnesium; this will raise pH)
>
> 1 part kelp meal (for micronutrients)

Mix with equal parts chipped leaf litter and trimming debris. Apply evenly four times from March through August (northern hemisphere) at the dripline (1½ to 3 pounds, or 0.7 to 1.4 kg, per tree, per application).

chapter six

PRUNING AND WEEDING

Pruning and weeding are often performed at the same time and both involve elements being *removed* from the orchard, so they are discussed together in this chapter.

BASICS

Trees cannot heal their wounds, not the way we can. Trees wall off damaged parts with a combination of tissue and chemicals to keep decay from spreading further. Then, if they have the energy, they grow past it. Trees don't heal, they *close*.[31] Every wound is permanent, and pruning inflicts wounds. Learn to do the least damage to prolong and enhance the lives of your trees.

Trees mount their defense against decay at the *branch bark ridge* and the *branch collar*. A swelling circles all the way around the base of a branch where it joins the trunk or another branch, and a ridge of bark pushes up in the angle between the two. These structures house the highest concentrations of the chemicals released in response to wounding. Pruning cuts made just outside the branch bark ridge and the branch collar supply the tree its best opportunity to *compartmentalize* the wound. Trees don't always succeed in preventing the spread of decay, even with properly made pruning cuts. The larger the diameter of the wound, the more time the tree needs to close it, and the tougher the battle to contain decay. Big cuts make hollow trees. Try to keep the diameter of pruning cut wounds to less than 2 inches (5.1 cm).

Tree and plant stems have buds along their lengths and at their ends. Either leaves or flowers emerge from the buds. Some of these buds are easily seen protruding from a twig; many more, called *latent buds*, are hidden under the bark. The visible buds on a stem are called *nodes* (typically located at the bases of leaves). The node at the end of a twig or stem is called the *terminal bud*. Lengths of stem between nodes are referred to as *internodal*. All pruning cuts occur either at a node, or between nodes, and a tree's response is different to each.

[31] Shigo, A.L. 1986. *A New Tree Biology: Facts, Photos, and Philosophies on Trees and Their Problems and Proper Care.* (Shigo and Trees Associates: Snohomish, Wash.).

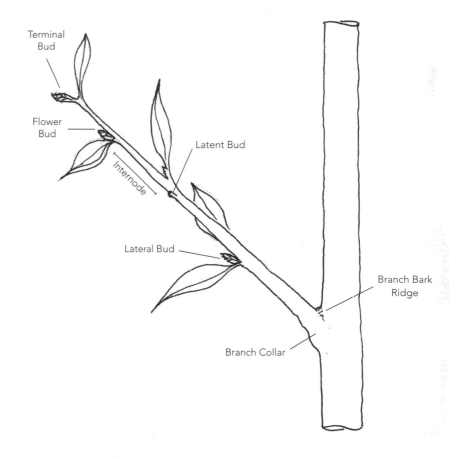

Anatomy of a Branch

Terminal Bud
Flower Bud
Internode
Latent Bud
Lateral Bud
Branch Bark Ridge
Branch Collar

The visible swelling of the branch collar around the base of this pawpaw tree branch should not be damaged during pruning.

Trees and plants begin all the food chains on the planet by making their own food. Green plant tissues, leaves for the most part, turn sunlight into sugar. Sugars are used for energy and are stored inside trees for later use. When we prune living, green leaves from a tree, its ability to make its own food is reduced. Do not remove more than 20 percent of a tree's canopy in a single pruning. Wait a year between prunings for young and mature fruit trees, longer for overmature trees.

The most stable structure for an *urban tree* (trees that live near people, buildings, roads, and other infrastructure) has a strong upright central leader with branch attachment angles of at least 45 degrees. Trees pruned into an open-vase shape will be developed to have four or five leaders. Branch collars are overlapping layers of wood formed by the central leader and the branch; the alternating layers form a strong union. Healthy branches with strong attachments are able to bear the weight of fruit. Young tree training and proper pruning helps to achieve this strong structure.

The best pruning cuts are the ones we never make. The best pruning cuts are the ones we prevent. The phrase, "Right tree, right place," cannot be repeated too often. Following the guidelines presented in previous chapters will prevent many pruning cuts. Choose trees grafted to the most appropriate rootstock for the home orchard's size to minimize future pruning. True dwarfing and semidwarf rootstocks go further toward keeping fruit trees at a manageable size than frequent encounters with loppers and saws. (Semidwarfs can still get pretty tall, though; keep in mind, 15 feet [4.6 m] is a *long* way up.)

After selecting fruit trees with the appropriate rootstock, decide what form and at what height to maintain the tree for its useful life. Young tree training and structural pruning begin the day the fruit trees are planted. Details on types of forms for temperate zone fruit and citrus trees are provided later in this chapter. For the first three or four years after planting a new tree, developing the mature form is the focus, fruit is not. Small pruning cuts made early in the lives of fruit trees can prevent the need to make large cuts later. Training young trees prevents pruning away a lot of green leafy growth during summer. Trees respond to excessive pruning of foliage by growing a lot more leaves to replace those removed. Proper pruning helps to limit this regrowth response, leaving more energy to put toward fruiting.

TOOLS

Have hand shears, loppers, a handsaw, pole pruner, and pole saw available to maintain the home orchard. Visually inspect all tools before, and clean tools after each use. Before and after the main seasonal pruning, thoroughly clean, sharpen, and lubricate all pruning tools. Learn to maintain tools properly to ensure their usefulness and your safety.

Hand shears, loppers, and pole pruners are basically the same tool with handles of different lengths—they are all shears. The way a pair of shears cuts a stem depends on the style of the shears: *anvil* or *bypass*. Anvil shears push the blade through the stem to a stop on a flat surface on the other handle, the anvil. Stems get crushed a little against the anvil, increasing injury. With bypass shears the blade "passes by" the stop, like a pair of scissors, and the stem is not crushed. Bypass shears are preferred; choose them when possible. Keeping blades properly sharpened is essential to minimizing pruning injury with either style of shears.

Pruning tools, such as hand shears (a), handsaws (b), loppers (c), pole pruners (d), and pole saws (e), should be kept sharp in order to minimize damage during cutting.

When using anvil-type shears, for a close cut, remember to position the blade closest to the part of the tree that is remaining.

ROOT PRUNING

The first pruning for a new tree is root pruning at planting time, when needed. Correcting the growth pattern of roots before the tree is planted prevents significant defects later: leaning trees, short-lived trees, stunted trees with poor vigor and few fruit, for example. Prune circling and severely kinked roots back to the point before the defect starts, or back to their point of origin—whichever comes first. The thicker the root and the closer to the trunk the circling begins, the more significant the defect. Make clean cuts with sharp blades; prune roots like they are shoots. Root pruning can slow growth of the above-ground parts of a tree, while new roots are growing to replace those removed. Only remove circling, girdling, or severely kinked roots—and do not prune excessively. Remove the cutoff portions from the root-ball before planting, if possible.

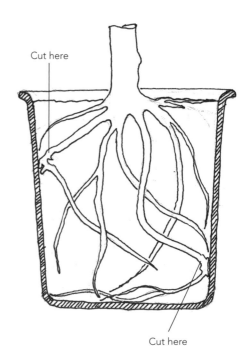

For healthy root establishment, prune thick, circling roots back to the point where they started circling.

CUTS

The terminal bud on a twig, stem, or the central leader suppresses the lateral and latent buds. When the terminal bud is removed through pruning, many of these buds will become active and grow. Pruning cuts made between nodes, that remove the terminal bud, are called *heading cuts*. The new stems resulting from the growth response to heading cuts are more weakly attached to the original stem and unlikely to form strong branch attachments on their own. Heading cuts result in a denser canopy with more poorly attached stems. Heading cuts can be used to shorten and decrease the vigor of stems that will be removed completely during a subsequent pruning.

Pruning cuts that remove a branch or twig at its point of origin, or at the juncture with another branch or twig at least one-third its diameter, are called *thinning cuts*. Proper thinning cuts avoid damaging the branch bark ridge and the branch collar. This type of cut doesn't cause a surge in the growth of latent buds, because the branch is removed entirely, or at the union with another branch large enough to take over the role of the terminal bud. Thinning cuts open up canopies, provide the optimum circumstance to close wounds, and minimize weakly attached lateral sprouts. Both heading and thinning cuts are used to train young fruit trees. The reason for pruning a branch or twig dictates which type of cut to use.

Terminal buds, found at the ends of shoots as pictured here, release hormones that inhibit the growth of lateral buds in a process called *apical dominance*, which is more pronounced in certain fruit trees. Removing terminal buds with heading cuts stimulates lateral bud growth and results in wider growth patterns.

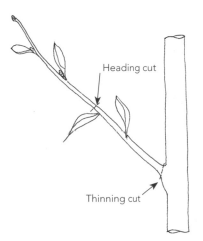

Heading cut

Thinning cut

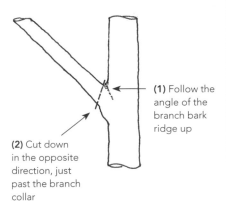

(1) Follow the angle of the branch bark ridge up

(2) Cut down in the opposite direction, just past the branch collar

Above right: Thinning (i.e., removing a branch) and heading (i.e., cutting back a branch) are two major types of pruning cuts.

Below right: Avoid making thinning cuts that are flush with adjoining branches or the trunk, which can damage the branch collar and branch bark ridge, leading to decay. At the same time, avoid cutting too far out and leaving stubs, which can delay wound closure. Instead, identify the branch collar and cut just outside of it. Sometimes the branch collar is not visibly pronounced, in which case **(1)** follow the angle created where the limbs meet, right up the middle, just past the branch bark ridge, and **(2)** angle the cut down in the opposite direction.

Above: A proper thinning cut made on a fruit tree just outside the branch collar and branch bark ridge.

Right: A proper heading cut made on a fruit tree. When making a heading cut above a bud, do so at a 45-degree angle so that the lower end of the cut is approximately in line with the tip of the bud and angles out towards the same direction the bud is facing. Encourage new growth to develop outward, rather than back towards the crown's interior, by cutting just above buds facing the outside edge of the canopy in the direction of desired growth.

Dead, Dying, Diseased, and Broken Branches

Let's look at the most important reasons for pruning trees. First, remove any and all dead, dying, diseased, or broken branches. Not sure if a branch is dead or alive? Deadwood is drier, lighter, and inflexible. The bark is dry, sometimes cracking, and sloughing off. Branch collars can appear more swollen than normal, because the dead branch is shrinking as it dries out. Check just under the bark for a green layer of tissue: For little twigs, scraping the surface with a fingernail will do; for bark a bit thicker, use the blade side of a pair of hand shears to flick a tiny piece of bark aside. A thin green layer underneath indicates the wood is alive. If it's brown or black, and dry, that part of the branch is dead. Check again, or more than once depending on the length of the branch, closer to its point of origin to determine if a portion of it is still live.

Suckers and Water Sprouts

Next, remove suckers and water sprouts. Suckers are leafy sprouts at the graft union or lower on a fruit tree. Suckers can also sprout right from roots close to the surface. Rootstocks are selected for vigor, and suckers left to grow can eventually dominate the growth of the entire tree. Cut suckers cleanly away at their point of origin. Water sprouts grow from the fruitwood; they are vigorous, upright leafy shoots. Remove water sprouts if they are crossing against other branches or shade the interior of the canopy, which will decrease fruit set. Water sprouts that will not be completely removed with the current pruning can be shortened with heading cuts to reduce their vigor. Water sprouts growing in a favorable spot can be kept and trained to become part of a tree's permanent structure, if needed—sometimes they replace broken branches, for example.

Above: Remove dead, dying, broken, or diseased branches whenever they are discovered.

Below: Unsure of whether or not a branch is dead? Live branches are flexible, while dead ones are brittle and snap easily. Scrape the surface of the bark in a smaller area than in this illustration, which was done for demonstration purposes. If it is green underneath, then the branch is still alive; if it is dark, then it can be removed.

Above: Remove suckers (left) and water sprouts (right) to focus a tree's energy on its most fruitful parts.

Below right: Included bark indicates a weak connection between stems, as shown in this union on a young pawpaw tree.

Scaffold Limbs

Branches that will be kept as integral parts of the fruit tree's basic form, trained to be the largest branches, are called *scaffold limbs*. Scaffold limbs should be well-spaced along and around the central leader, and not closer together than 6 to 8 inches (15.2 to 20.3 cm) on a young tree. Their angle of attachment should be at least 45 degrees and not greater than 60 degrees. None of them should have a diameter greater than half that of the trunk.

Codominant Stems

Remove or shorten *codominant stems*. Thick stems, growing in a strongly upright direction, with a narrow angle of attachment to the central leader are called codominant stems. They're branches that want to be trunks, too. Vigorous, with a diameter close or equal to the central leader's, codominant stems are the building blocks of very significant structural defects in trees. Left to grow, the codominant stem is no longer a branch. The tree now has two leaders with a narrow angle between them. As each leader grows and gains girth, they push against each other and pressure builds in that narrow *crotch* where they are joined. As the attachment becomes increasingly weak, bark from each

stem is compressed inside the crotch. *Included bark* adds to this defect and indicates a weak union prone to breakage. Prune out or shorten codominant stems as early as possible during young tree training.

Small twigs with narrow crotches can be corrected with spreaders and trained to grow into a wider angle of attachment. Remove codominant stems already too large to be retrained at their point of origin. Examine both stems and choose the straightest, most upright, and most vigorous of the two to be the central leader. Codominant stems so large they cannot be completely removed in a single pruning can be shortened with a heading cut to reduce their vigor.[32] A combination of heading cuts and training with spreaders can be used to correct some codominant stems.

Additional Pruning

Additional pruning treatments for fruit trees are designed to maximize the number, size, and quality of fruit. Some fruit trees, such as figs, bear only on branches grown during the current season. Others fruit on last year's wood, like peaches, and still others bear fruit on short stubby twigs called *spurs* for many years (apples and pears). Know which growth season's wood a tree fruits on before pruning.

[32] Gilman, E.F. 2002. *An Illustrated Guide to Pruning.* (Delmar Thompson Learning: Albany, N.Y.).

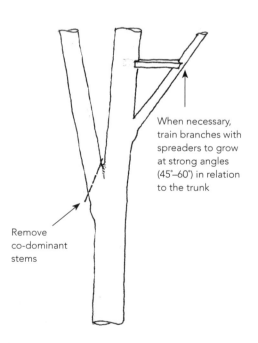

When necessary, train branches with spreaders to grow at strong angles (45°–60°) in relation to the trunk

Remove co-dominant stems

FORMS

Modified Central Leader

Any home orchard fruit tree can be trained to a *modified central leader form*, but it's most often used for apples, pears, and nut trees. One trunk is maintained at a designated height with heading cuts, and four to eight scaffold limbs, spaced evenly along and around the trunk, are developed. The modified central leader form helps to keep semidwarf temperate zone fruit trees to a manageable height, and also keeps fruiting lower in the canopy. The central leader is headed back to a lateral branch to maintain height; scaffolds are trained with spreaders and heading cuts to create wide angles of attachment. Water sprouts and codominant stems are removed. Young tree training extends through the first three years. Trees beginning to bear fruit, from four to ten years old, will need less pruning. As trees mature, however, the modified central leader form requires using increasing numbers of heading cuts to maintain their height and spread.

Open Vase

Open vase form trees are pruned to have a short trunk of 18 to 24 inches (45.7 to 61 cm). Four or five scaffold limbs are selected and grow to become multiple leaders, radiating from the top of the short trunk. Scaffolds should be 4 to 6 inches (10.2 to 15.2 cm) apart with attachment angles of 45 to 60 degrees. This fruit tree form, typically used for peaches and nectarines, brings maximum sunlight into the entire canopy of a very low, very wide tree. Open vase trees must begin to be trained at planting. Pruning to maintain this form is needed throughout the life of the tree to keep the center open, to head back overextended lateral limbs, and to remove older lateral branches curving down and growing toward the ground (called *hooks*). Open vase form trees bear the weight of fruit very well, have good distribution of fruit through the canopy, and are easy to work. Each tree, however, takes up a lot more space than a comparable tree pruned to a modified central leader form.

Citrus and Subtropicals

Citrus trees, and many other subtropicals, are pruned differently than temperate zone fruit trees. Size is easily managed with rootstock selection. Citrus bark baking in the sun gets damaged, and so citrus canopies must shade the main branches and trunk. The primary task in pruning citrus is to remove deadwood, which consists of small twiggy growth for the most part. An occasional vigorous shoot, extending well past the edge of a mature canopy, will need to be headed back, but in other circumstances, use thinning cuts for citrus. Pruning the perimeter of citrus trees, lightly, to permit a *little* more sunlight to penetrate into the *outer* portion of the canopy, can improve quantity and quality of fruit. Keep branches from dragging the ground, or brushing against fences, walls, or other trees. Prune citrus trees so that the trunk is the only part of the tree that contacts the ground. This practice is useful for controlling insects. (More on insects later.)

Espalier

Espalier is a formal style of training used to grow fruit trees onto a flat, vertical surface, such as a fence or a wall. Trunks and limbs are attached to the surface and trained to grow flat against it; symmetrical and ornamental patterns can be created. Training to espalier form begins by planting a new sapling 6 to 8 inches (15.2 to 20.3 cm) from the wall or fence. The location for the espalier must receive full sun. Spreaders, heading cuts, and tying stems to the surface are used to train fruit trees to grow into this flat, formal shape. Apples and pears on dwarfing rootstocks are frequently chosen for espalier. A very high-maintenance form, espalier is a way to use all available space to grow fruit trees.

Below: Pruning forms best suited for fruit trees include: central leader, modified central leader, and open vase. The central leader form produces a tree with a single, dominant trunk with strong lateral connections. Modified central leader has a shorter, central trunk branching off into multiple scaffolds. Open vase allows more sunlight in the canopy, a wider structure, and less vulnerability to disease due to its many branchings (some of which may survive should others succumb, whereas a central leader has only a single trunk). Choose the form that best suits the tree, conditions, and desired accessibility to harvest.

Central Leader

Modified Central Leader

Open Vase

Espaliered trees have striking appearances and can be used as living fence structures. Trellises provide excellent training support and trained trees can be planted in narrow spaces or grown in containers successfully.

THINNING

Fruit thinning is a small-scale pruning chore with big benefits at harvest time. Thinning results in larger-size fruit, with better color and flavor from increased exposure to sunlight. Fruit thinning reduces trees' tendency to *alternate bear*—lots of fruit one year, almost none the next. Thinning reduces limb breakage from heavy crop loads and can decrease the spread of some diseases. Some fruit trees are self-thinning: cherry, fig, pomegranate, citrus, and nut trees drop a portion of their immature fruit. Thinning is needed for the stone fruits, such as peaches and apricots, as well as apples and pears. Time thinning carefully; don't be too early, or too late. Thin stone fruits when they are ¾ to 1 inch (1.9 to 2.5 cm) in diameter, apples and pears at ½ to 1 inch (1.3 to 2.5 cm), or four to six weeks after full bloom. Thin small stone fruits, such as apricots and plums, to 2 to 4 inches (5.1 to 10.2 cm) apart on the branch, larger ones, such as peaches and nectarines, to 3 to 5 inches (7.6 to 12.7 cm). Apples and pears bloom in clusters; thin each cluster to just one or two fruits. Keep the biggest fruit in each cluster, and space fruit to 6 to 8 inches (15.2 to 20.3 cm) apart.

Thinning can be done by hand or using a pole. By hand is a slow but accurate method best used on fruit trees kept low enough to reach through the canopy fairly easily. Use hand shears and leave the stem on the tree—just remove the fruit. Lighten the fruit load more toward the ends of branches; leave a greater number of fruits closer to the trunk. Remove damaged, disfigured, very small, and doubles (two fruits fused together) first. Pole-thinning is faster, not so accurate, and easier with taller trees. Cover the end of the pole with tape or cloth to reduce damage. Extending the pole up into the canopy, strike fruit clusters, to knock a portion of the immature fruit out of the tree.

MATURE TREE REJUVENATION

Rejuvenating a mature fruit tree begins with pruning. Attempting to prune a large, old, neglected tree is a daunting task, but the rewards of tackling it may be well worth the trouble. Before getting started, ask some questions. What type of fruit tree is it and what variety? Before even picking up a pair of hand shears, perform a thorough visual inspection of the tree. First, find the graft union and make sure the tree is not just the rootstock that has taken over. If the tree has fruit, pick one and give it a taste; worms, disease, and damage aside, try to assess its quality.

Now, check the tree for significant structural defects: tears on the trunk from past limb failures, dead and broken branches, hollows in large limbs or the trunk, or both. Don't forget to look down; use a rake to move leaf litter aside. Examine the basal flare and the root crown area. Look for damage and decay on *buttress roots*, the large anchoring roots rising to the surface to meet the basal flare. Tree roots typically decay from the underside first. A soft, spongy buttress root that smashes apart with a boot heel and smells like mushrooms has rotted all the way through, from the bottom up. Speaking of mushrooms—any visible growing from the surface of roots, or as "shelves" on the basal flare or trunk, is an indicator of advanced decay in trees. Discovering any one of the above-described defects ought to give one pause before attempting to rejuvenate an old fruit tree. The presence of multiple structural defects increases the hazard of working in or near such a tree. Do not prune or try to remove a hazardous tree. Call in a certified arborist to provide an evaluation and risk assessment of the tree, and ask for some advice about what course of action to pursue (check with the International Society of Arboriculture to find a certified arborist in your area).

To Rejuvenate a Tree

If after a visual check, it's just a big old tree with a thicket full of water sprouts in the center, and a sparse showing of fruit high up on the outside of the canopy, rejuvenating the tree through pruning might be a worthwhile endeavor.

1. To begin, remove all deadwood and suckers. Prune deciduous trees while dormant, when branching patterns are easier to see. Try to visualize the best structure to develop.

2. Use thinning cuts to reduce the tree's height and open up the canopy; help sunlight reach the lower branches. Mature tree rejuvenation is the one time making larger cuts is the preferred method. When in doubt, always ask an expert for advice based on a site visit.

3. A saw will be needed to remove branches larger than 2 inches (5.1 cm) in diameter. To prevent tearing bark while removing a large limb, make a series of three cuts. First, identify the location of the branch bark ridge and the branch collar; next, plan where to make each of the three cuts described below *before* making them. The *back cut* is made on the underside of the limb to be removed, 8 to 12 inches (20.3 to 30.5 cm) away from the branch collar, as though leaving a stub. Cut up about one-third of the way through. Make the top cut 2 inches (5.1 cm) farther out on the branch from the back cut. Cut all the way through and let the branch fall away. (Away from you, from everybody below, from other branches—in other words, clear the area ahead of time.) Now remove the stub left behind with the *final cut*, making it at the proper place and angle to preserve the branch bark ridge and the branch collar.

Apples, pears, and citrus exhibit the best response to mature tree rejuvenation pruning. Spread this severe pruning strategy over a period of two or three years, or up to six

for particularly old trees, and start working from the top and outside of the canopy down. Remember, pruning during dormancy stimulates growth, but summer pruning removes green growth, restricting or dwarfing the tree.

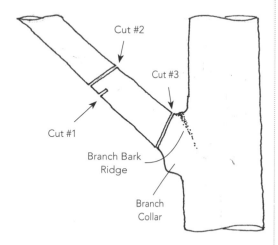

Cut #2

Cut #3

Cut #1

Branch Bark Ridge

Branch Collar

Left: To prevent tearing damage when removing large limbs, follow these steps in sequence: **(1)** On the underside of the branch, cut about one-third of the way up, 8 to 12 inches (20.3 to 30.5 cm) away from the branch collar. **(2)** Next, cut from the top all the way through the limb about 2 inches (5.1 cm) farther away from the branch collar than the first cut. **(3)** Finally, remove the stub without disturbing the branch collar or branch bark ridge.

Below: Even ancient trees can be rejuvenated through pruning, as illustrated by this centuries-old apple tree.

TOPPING

Topping is a slang term used to describe *indiscriminant* heading cuts made to reduce the height of trees. Topping has the opposite of its intended effect and encourages trees to replace the growth removed with poorly attached stems prone to breakage and failure. Cuts are made internodally, so wound closure is poor and opportunity for decay to move into the central leader and major laterals is greatly increased. Topping fruit trees moves their energy toward shoot growth and away from fruit set, and may expose bark to sunscald injury. Topping is a detrimental treatment for any type of tree and should not be performed. Reducing mature tree height is a process done in carefully thought-out phases. Absolutely steer clear of commercial tree trimmers who offer topping as a "service."

RULES OF THUMB

Say no to paints and dressings: Trees close their own wounds very well when pruning cuts are made adjacent the branch bark ridge and the branch collar, without damaging them. Despite these facts, pruning paints or wound dressings are still sold at garden centers and home improvement stores. Advertisements for these products push the notion that painting pruning cuts promotes "healing." Not only does science not bear this idea out, but it refutes it altogether. Pruning paints and wound dressings do more harm than good. These products hamper wound closure by plastering pathogens against the wound, by keeping the cut moist, and by blocking out air and light. Studies have shown increased decay patterns for painted versus unpainted wounds.[33] Do not paint pruning cuts.

Use young tree training: Closing pruning wounds greater than 2 inches (5.1 cm) in diameter challenges trees. They need more time to close larger wounds, which gives disease and decay organisms an opportunity to move in and become established inside wood. Use young tree training to avoid future large diameter cuts. Keep up with seasonal pruning chores, so water sprouts and suckers don't grow thicker than 2 inches (5.1 cm). When larger pruning cuts cannot be avoided, make them during the season that gives the tree its best chance to close them before attack by pathogens. Best timing for large pruning cuts depends on the type of fruit tree, local climate, and regional pest pressures. Check with the local Agricultural Extension office for this information.

Plan ahead: Carefully think about the desired structure and whether or not the cuts made achieve this. Picture a bird's-eye view and space branches evenly around the trunk. Remem-

Why Prune?

Trees survive without human-inflicted pruning; just look outside for countless examples of Mother Nature doing the job just fine. In order to maximize health, fruit set, longevity, and aesthetics in an orchard setting, however, pruning is used as a tool. Some of the most direct benefits of pruning include:

- ✓ Strengthening tree structure to prevent future limb and trunk breakage
- ✓ Improving air circulation and access to sunlight
- ✓ Making harvest more accessible
- ✓ Training the tree to take a particular shape (e.g., shorter, wider, thinner, espalier)
- ✓ Removing dead or diseased tree branches
- ✓ Thinning fruit for larger, healthier fruit

[33] Shigo, A. L. 1986. *A New Tree Biology: Facts, Photos, and Philosophies on Trees and Their Problems and Proper Care.* (Shigo and Trees Associates: Snohomish, WA).

When to Prune

Prune trees of broken, damaged, or diseased branches at planting, or whenever they are detected; however, consider waiting a month or two for the tree to recover from the stress of transplant before making additional cuts.

Late winter or early spring is generally an excellent time to prune in order to stimulate growth during the spring and summer months. Pruning trees when they are dormant has the advantage of fewer insects and diseases in the surrounding environment (if pruned in winter), and for deciduous trees, greater visibility of branch structure when leaves are not present. Moreover, because trees store energy reserves when they are dormant, making cuts at this time allows them to use those reserves on fewer, more focused branch structures in the spring, resulting in more concentrated growth patterns. So, make most structural pruning cuts when trees are dormant to stimulate vigorous growth during the growing season.

In cold-winter climates, dormant pruning should occur in early spring after the last frost and before bud break, except for apricots (which should not be pruned at all when dormant because it makes them susceptible to a disease called *Eutypa*). For warm-winter climates, dormant pruning can occur between the time when deciduous trees lose their leaves and before bud break.

In the late spring and summer, trees expend their stored energy on vigorous shoot growth. If extensive summer pruning removes branches that contain these shoots and leaves, the trees will not have enough energy reserves available to make up for the loss and will thus go into a period of slower growth. For this reason, practice summer pruning to slow down growth and promote dwarfing. Focus summer pruning on removing suckers and water sprouts, and making thinning cuts aimed at increasing sun exposure for other parts of the tree or improving fruit quality. In cold-winter climates, avoid late summer or autumn pruning. New growth requires sufficient time to completely harden off before the first frost; otherwise, tender shoots may be damaged.

Become an expert in pruning by tracking your results and learning from experience—your orchard will benefit greatly!

ber that branches and limbs don't rise with a growing tree (i.e., a knot in a tree will remain at the same elevation regardless of how tall the tree grows), so any cut you make will remain at that elevation for the life of the tree. Allow low branching for easier access to fruit. And remember to chip and return all disease-free pruned branches to the orchard floor with mulch to preserve soil nutrients.

Think before you cut: Plan pruning maintenance for fruit trees, both short and long term. Know the reason to make each cut, before making it. About to cut through a branch and you don't know why? Don't cut until you know.

WEEDING

Just like death and taxes, weeds in the orchard are guaranteed. Make weed control a part of routine orchard maintenance. Home orchards with regular weed control practices suffer the minor annoyance of an occasional weed, but those without any often surrender to a tree-stunting, fruit-robbing menace.

Plants are not "good" or "bad" in and of themselves. The term *weed* is used in this book without any derogatory implication—and only refers to the commonly accepted definition that a weed is a plant that we do not want where it is growing because it has a robust nature, capable of displacing other plants that we do want. Typical orchard weeds can be annuals or perennials. An annual completes its life cycle, seed to seed, in a single growing season. Perennials live longer than two growing seasons and produce seeds more than once. Orchard weeds can be broadleaf plants, such as dandelion, or grasses, such as Bermuda grass.

Weeds hamper the growth and productivity of fruit trees because they compete, very successfully, for the same resources: water, soil nutrients, and space in the root zone. Weeds are short-lived compared to fruit trees, but they are more nimble. They counter their short lives with a multitude of seeds that remain viable for decades. For example, a single plant of common purslane, an edible "weed" valued by many for its culinary uses, can set more than 240,000 seeds. Those seeds can lie dormant, but still viable, in the soil for more than twenty years. Soils hold literally millions of dormant weed seeds that need only a second or two of exposure to sunlight to germinate.

A thicket of weeds surrounding a fruit tree shortens the length of yearly shoot growth and decreases the quantity of fruit set, and the size of those fruits. The effect of competing with weeds is especially damaging to newly planted young trees. The rapid growth rate of shoots in young trees should be encouraged to build a strong structure for fruit bearing. Shoot growth for new trees establishing themselves among heavy weeds averages just 25 percent of that grown by similar trees planted in a mulched orchard. When the weeds are removed, young trees dwarfed by this competition do not necessarily regain their vigor and attain a normal stature later. Keep all vegetation at least 3 feet (0.9 m) away from newly planted fruit trees. Maintain this weed-free circle throughout their useful lives.

Plan ahead to wage the battle against orchard weeds. Evaluate the weed management strategies outlined in this chapter, and choose a combination best adapted to the local climate and weed population. Beyond minimizing weeds in the orchard, a weed control method should not harm trees or soil. Weed control should not create or exacerbate soil erosion, or soil compaction. It should not damage the soil's infiltration rate, or its content of organic matter. It should not have a positive effect on the weed seed bank, and it should not compete with the fruit trees for resources. Weed control methods outlined in this book are organic-method compatible, and do not promote the use of synthetic chemical herbicides.

Coarse wood chips make for excellent mulch and are often available for free or low-cost from tree trimmers or local recycling programs. Recycling is the key to a healthy ecosystem!

Mulches

A thick layer of biodegradable mulch, such as wood chips, controls weeds by blocking sunlight exposure to seeds. Keep mulch layers 4 to 6 inches (10.2 to 15.2 cm) thick. After excellent weed control, the benefits of mulching the orchard floor are many. Mulches prevent soil erosion, improve infiltration rates, and help build healthy soils by increasing organic matter and nutrients in the root zone. Fruit trees grown in mulched orchards have improved shoot growth, and fruit quantity and quality.

The downside to mulching the *entire* orchard floor? Mulches decompose and need to be replenished (use recycled materials when possible). Check the depth of the mulch layer at least once a year. Moving wheelbarrows and other garden equipment through mulch can be tedious. It's tough to maintain a consistent layer of mulch on a steep slope. In wet climates, mulches can hold too much water, or decompose too rapidly to justify their expense. In dry climates, they can be combustible. (Mineral mulches are an alternative for fire-prone and desert locales.) Sometimes a mulch layer harbors rodents. The benefits of mulching the orchard floor outweigh the disadvantages most of the time. Mulches are a good choice for orchards that are spray irrigated. Keep mulch at least a few inches away from tree trunks in all circumstances. Supplement weed control in mulched orchards by hand-pulling or spot-spraying isolated weeds.

Cover Crops (Living Mulches)

Cover crops, or living mulches, suppress weeds by outcompeting them. Cover crops grow a carpet over the orchard floor to shut weeds out. Commonly grown in the aisles between rows of fruit trees (called the *middles*), living mulches often provide habitat for beneficial insects. They also increase the soil's organic matter content with time. Legumes, plants in the bean family, harvest nitrogen from the air to meet as much as one-third of their own need for this nutrient. Using legumes as a cover crop increases the amount of available nitrogen in the root zone. Living mulches prevent soil erosion. Cool-season annual grasses are frequently used as cover crops because they die back in the summer, when water and nutrient needs of fruit trees peak. These grasses are mowed at the end of their growing season, and the clippings left on the orchard floor as a mulch. Cover crops do compete with fruit trees, however, and shoot growth rates and fruiting are affected in orchards maintained with them. Living mulches used for weed control are best for climates where they will not need irrigation. Furthermore, with some fruits—apples for example—legume cover crops are not recommended because they add too much nitrogen, promoting shoot growth over fruiting. Living mulches have also sometimes been shown to increase vole populations.

Not only is weeding by hand an environmentally friendly method, it can provide a source of horticultural therapy, which has been shown to decrease stress and enhance overall productivity.[34]

[34] Worden E., T. Frohne, and J. Sullivan. 2004. "Horticultural Therapy." University of Florida IFAS Extension Publication #ENH970.

Cultivation

Cultivation is the practice of shallow-tilling the orchard floor to uproot weeds. Repeated at regular intervals through the growing season, this method of weed control eliminates annual weeds very well—perennial weeds, not as well. Using a power tiller to cut up and toss around chunks of perennial weeds, such as Bermuda grass and johnsongrass, just redistributes them across the orchard floor. Cultivation accelerates soil erosion, and damages soil structure and infiltration rates. It decreases organic matter content in the root zone over time. Cultivation also stirs up the seed bank, essentially setting up the next crop of weeds, while controlling the current one. Using gas-powered tillers leaves a carbon footprint that will need to be repeated two to four times through a single growing season. The potential to damage fruit tree roots with tilling equipment is ever-present. Despite the drawbacks, cultivation is the most prevalent weed control method used today in commercial organic orchards, and cultivation has been used in agriculture for millennia, all over the globe, for both planting and weeding crops.

In order to avoid the environmental damage from mechanical cultivation, especially in smaller home orchard settings, removal of weeds by hand, using tools to uproot weeds, is a most effective, environmentally friendly method. Doing so also allows one to become more familiar and knowledgeable with the site, after getting up close and personal with different portions and layers of the orchard soil. This can benefit other aspects of orchard maintenance and care.

Learn what kinds of weeds are growing in the orchard. Seize the opportunity to eradicate them, especially perennials, *before* planting fruit trees whenever possible. Once the orchard is planted, maintain a schedule of weed control. Growing fruit trees without controlling weeds results in smaller trees, with fewer fruits.

Specialty weed control methods are also available to supplement any of the primary strategies. For example, non-toxic, organic herbicides include clove oil, vinegar, and citric acid. These are called *contact herbicides*, which means when sprayed on, they kill the leaves they touch. They are not systemic; they do not move inside plants to kill the roots. Garden centers and home improvement stores may carry premixed formulations of these alternatives, or research proven, organic options and recipes online.

Weeds Wanted!

In areas prone to severe erosion due to wind or water runoff, some plants may be beneficial around fruit trees to anchor in soil and preserve root-zone topsoil. When FTPF donated and planted more than a thousand fruit trees with the Hopi tribe of northeastern Arizona, where high desert winds erode sandy soils at will, it was discovered that leaving some anchoring plants near newly planted trees aided in keeping valuable soil in place and ultimately optimizing survival rates. An exception to the weeding rule can be made in such situations. Yet another illustration that while there are always guiding principles that steer us toward successful strategies, every planting has unique needs and properties that should be evaluated on a case-by-case basis. A good reminder to think outside the box!

In rare cases where high winds erode a planting site significantly, an exception to the weed removal rule may be made as native flora will help stabilize the soil around the tree.

Companion Planting and Permaculture

In nature, plants grow aside one another, often symbiotically, despite limited resources. For a more natural landscape, consider planting select understory *companion plants* that complement fruit trees while providing additional harvest opportunities. The practice of *permaculture*, which involves holistic agricultural designs to mimic natural ecosystems, often employs closely knit plantings of edible crops and fruit trees. While there may still be competition for resources, if designed properly, the complementary benefits of companion plantings can provide a robust and well-rounded orchard setting, especially in urban settings where space may be scarce. Many communities offer permaculture classes and seminars that serve as useful introductions to design principles.

Once a young tree is established in its new surroundings, symbiotic plants may be planted near the tree according to established permaculture practices. These understory onions are said to provide protection against peach leaf curl.

chapter seven

PREVENTION, TROUBLESHOOTING, AND CONTROLS

An ounce of prevention *really is* worth a pound of cure, so although this chapter offers specific information about dealing with the organisms and conditions that harm fruit trees, it begins with strategies to prevent them in the first place.

IN EVERY SITUATION, FTPF RECOMMENDS using organic, humane control methods only, for the least invasive, most sustainable outcome possible. Toxic chemicals upset the natural balance of the home orchard, and do more damage than good.[35] They can also harm beneficial insects, other wildlife, and humans. Every situation has a gentle, Earth-friendly solution, and this chapter identifies many such strategies for the most common ailments.

RIGHT TREE, RIGHT PLACE

Choose the fruit trees, both fruitwood and rootstock, that are best adapted to the orchard's climate and soil. Trees poorly adapted to their environment spend energy struggling to survive. They do not produce abundant fruit and are more vulnerable to attack by pathogenic organisms. Find out about the locally prevalent nonbeneficial insects and diseases to help choose the most resistant cultivars available. To know when something is wrong, learn what *right* looks like. What does health look like for leaves, flowers, fruit, and bark, for each kind of fruit tree in the orchard?

Plant trees in full sun with good air circulation, at the proper depth. Follow correct irrigation practices. Wood-boring insects can smell drought-stressed trees. Overly wet soils not only deprive roots of oxygen, they grow anaerobic organisms; some of them are pathogens. Fertilize trees with the correct amount per application, and at the right time during the growing season. Control nitrogen levels. Excess nitrogen promotes leaves at the expense of fruit; those big, floppy, extra-green leaves are very attractive to foliage-feeding insects. Time pruning correctly as well. Prune at the right time for each type of fruit tree growing in the orchard.

For example, do not prune apricots during the dormant season. They must be pruned at least six weeks before the first rains come to decrease infection by Eutypa fungus.

Watch out for signs and symptoms. Walk through the orchard, looking the trees over; notice the atypical. A *sign* is the presence or direct evidence of a nonbeneficial insect, mite, or pathogen, like wood-borer frass (sawdust), fungal conks, and insect egg masses. A *symptom* is the visible expression of the tree's response to harmful organisms: wilting or discolored leaves, stunted growth, sap oozing from bark. Symptoms for different maladies often look the same. This combination of signs and symptoms needs to be observed and identified before taking any action to remedy the situation—indeed, positive identification is required to determine if any action is needed at all.

A fruit tree's best defense against harmful organisms and pathogens is prevention through proper tree selection, planting, irrigation, fertilization, pruning, and cleanup—in other words, staying strong and healthy.

[35] In fact, synthetic pesticide use and overuse is a relatively new concept, emerging around the time of World War II, and has negative consequences that haven't even been fully understood yet. For thousands of years prior (i.e., most of human agricultural history), synthetic pesticides were not part of the agricultural landscape and more organic rearing methods were considered conventional.

Fungal growths or conks, like on this peach tree branch **(right)** and especially at the base of trunks **(above)**, are indicators of internal decay.

ORCHARD CLEANUP

To limit the advance of harmful organisms at the beginning of the next growing season, clean up the orchard during autumn. For deciduous fruit trees, rake up and remove fallen leaves. For citrus trees, prune back any branches that are touching other structures, such as fences or houses, to prevent crawling organisms from finding a way onto the tree. For all fruit trees, pick up and remove dead fruit, both fallen and still attached to limbs. Prune out and remove any dead twigs and branches. All of this late-season litter can be composted. If the compost pile is maintained to reach a temperature of 150°F to 160°F (66°C to 71°C) for three to four days, the resulting compost will be free of diseases and weed seeds and can be returned to the orchard floor. (Please see the Recommended Reading list for references on composting.) After the orchard cleanup is complete, spray an organic dormant oil and fungicide to prevent infection next spring. Specifics about these sprays, and other control methods, can be found in the next section and the tables at the end of the chapter.

Above: Proper cleanup eliminates breeding grounds for pathogens.

Left: Spoiled or damaged tree fruit serves as a valuable source of nutrients and micronutrients for the garden and may be composted to nourish the next generation of plants.

INSECTS, MITES, AND NEMATODES

The insects, mites, and nematodes that commonly damage fruit and fruit trees can be sorted by the types of action they make when feeding.

Sap-sucking insects and mites pierce foliage or stems and suck out plant juices to sustain themselves. Sucking types include aphids, mealybugs, scale, psyllids, leaf-hoppers, and spider mites. Thrips often infest flowers, but they can also be found on tender new leaves and shoots, and occasionally on small fruit. Thin and black, thrips move quickly and are about the size of the eye of a needle. They feed by rasping the surface of plant tissues, and then sucking up the released juices.

Symptoms of damage caused by these sucking organisms are most noticeable on foliage. Leaves may look discolored, or distorted by puckering or curling. Leaves sucked dry will turn brown and fall from the tree. Aphid populations tend to peak in early spring on tender new growth. Spider mites favor dry, dusty conditions; they can be carried on the wind. They cause the most damage to drought-stressed plants and trees. Sucking insects and mites can be vectors, carriers of other plant diseases, especially viruses. Fungal and bacterial diseases may also be transmitted to fruit trees by sucking insects and mites. Aphids vector the largest number of different plant diseases, thrips the fewest.

Aphids are among the most harmful organisms for fruit trees as they are vectors of many diseases. Common aphids pictured here include the green peach aphid **(above)**, black cherry aphid **(below left)**, and winged aphid **(below right)**. When host tree resources deteriorate, some species can give birth to winged offspring who then migrate to a healthier host.

Aphids

Mealybugs

Common sucking insects that harm fruit trees are shown here.

Spider mite

Cottony cushion scale

Sucking Insects

Sucking insects and mites excrete a sticky-sweet goo called *honeydew*. Even though each individual insect or mite is tiny, the whole population can secrete sufficient quantities to coat leaves with a sticky shine, and the excess drips down onto any surface below the trees (picnic tables, sidewalks, car windshields). A fungus, called *black sooty mold*, lives on honeydew, cloaking the sticky leaves with a fine black dust. All of this is unsightly but not harmful to foliage and can be washed off with a hose-end spray nozzle.

Ants love to eat honeydew, too. They farm aphids, mealybugs, soft scales, and whiteflies to harvest their honeydew. Ants will bring sucking insects into fruit trees, particularly citrus, and then guard their herds by killing beneficial insects, such as lacewings. Excluding ants from

Citrus psyllid

citrus trees provides some control of sucking insect populations. Prune citrus trees so that the only point of contact with the ground for each tree is the trunk. (Ants can't jump.) Branches must not touch the ground, walls, fences, or other trees.

Discouraging the conditions that these insects and mites prefer can help to decrease their numbers and impact in the orchard. Fruit thinning, pruning at the proper time, and following the orchard cleanup guidelines described above will help. Preventing drought stress and excess nitrogen levels does, too. The soft-bodied sucking insects have a host of natural enemies: lacewings, lady beetles, minute pirate bugs, parasitic wasps, and many types of birds, especially finches, enjoy snacks of aphids and psyllids, too. Encourage conditions favorable to these beneficial organisms in order to provide a line of protection. (See photos for examples.)

A minute pirate bug having a meal

Lady beetle devouring an aphid

Parasitic wasp laying eggs in a tarnished plant bug carcass

Lacewing larvae ingesting harmful insect nymphs …

and in adult form

Left: Most insects are not harmful to fruit trees. In fact, many, such as bees and wasps, are absolutely essential as pollinators and predators of nonbeneficial insects. Indiscriminant toxic pesticides should always be avoided to maintain a healthy orchard balance.

Below: This fecal trail in a citrus leaf is an early sign of leaf miner larva infestation.

Chewing Insects

Chewing insects eat foliage or fruit, or both. Moths and beetles whose larvae (caterpillars and grubs) eat leaves and fruit are included in this group. Leaf-eaters include snails and slugs, earwigs, tent caterpillars, leaf miners, and leaf rollers. Damage to foliage by these types of insects is similar and easy to discern, except for leaf miners. This type of insect chews out all or part of the underside of leaves, leaving just the veins and the waxy coating on the surface, giving leaves a skeletonized appearance. Fruit-eating insects are the most difficult to control and cause the most damage to fruit crops: codling moth, plum curculio, apple maggots, cherry fruit fly, and oriental fruit moth, to name a few. The adult females of these species may lay eggs on the foliage, on the fruit surface, or insert eggs into the fruit. The larvae crawl to the fruit, bore into it if they are already on the surface, or hatch inside and feed.

For apples and pears, exclusionary protection from many fruit-eating insects such as codling moths, in prone areas, can be achieved by thinning clusters down to one fruit, and then covering them with standard paper lunch bags. Cut a slit in the bottom, folded end of the bag, large enough to slip the fruit through when it is

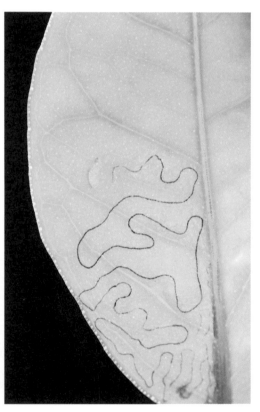

golf ball–size, or ½ to ¾ inch (1.3 to 1.9 cm) in diameter. Allow the slit to close over the stem and staple the top of the bag firmly shut. Ripeness may be checked, being careful to restaple the bag afterward. Bag as many fruits as desired. Research shows that doing so not only protects them from common insects and diseases, but it also results in fewer defects.[35] In fact, some Asian commercial growers use a similar bagging method to grow premium fruits. For red apples, remove bags about a week prior to harvest to allow for color development.

Wood-Boring Insects

Wood-boring insects are the larvae of beetles and moths that chew their way into branches and trunks, instead of leaves or fruit. Healthy trees can fend off borer assaults by pushing sap into entry holes and smothering the

[36] Bessin, R. 2003. "Bagging Apples: Alternative Pest Management for Hobbyists." University of Kentucky Cooperative Extension Service. ENTFACT-218.

borers. Older trees, drought-stressed trees, or trees already in distress from other insects or diseases, often lack the vigor to respond and successfully repel wood borers. Borers can kill a fruit tree. Prevention is the best strategy against wood-boring insects. Maintain healthy trees to keep stress low and energy high. Vigilant end-of-season orchard cleanup and subsequent organic dormant oil spray applications decrease the number of overwintered wood borer eggs. Protect fruit tree trunks from injury, especially sunscald (described in the Environmental Disorders section.) Root-knot nematodes are microscopic worms that bore into tree roots and disrupt their function. Infested trees are stunted, do not have good fruit set, and live a shorter life span than is typical. Nematodes prefer sandy soils. They are very difficult to control, so find out if root-knot nematode inhabits the orchard's soil before planting, and select resistant rootstocks.

Root-knot nematodes are microscopic worms that attack tree roots, leading to stunted growth and deformities, as shown in these citrus tree roots. Choose resistant rootstocks and select sites with uninfected soil.

Above: Organic dormant oil mixtures can be purchased or made at home according to your favorite online recipe using non-GMO oils, biodegradable soap, and water. Spray the mixture onto dormant tree branches and trunks until they are wet, on days without extreme heat, freezing conditions, or precipitation. The oil works to prevent overwintering eggs and fungal spores from developing. Take one winter afternoon to apply a dormant oil and make a world of difference during the growing season.

Left: After prevention, the first line of defense against many unwanted organisms using organic, humane control methods is to physically remove them. Both small and large insects can be picked off, brushed off (by hand or with a paintbrush), or hosed off. A slight shaking of a branch on this pawpaw tree is enough to scare this damaging stinkbug away. Know the feeding pattern of the organism. Snails, for example, feed at night, and can easily be removed all at once with a flashlight or a bright moon.

DISEASES

Diseases that afflict fruit trees can be caused by bacteria, fungi, or viruses. They can be vectored by insects and mites. Inoculums can be introduced to trees by birds and honeybees—or boots, pruning tools, and tires. *Vascular* diseases of trees clog the movement of water, nutrients, and sugars through live wood; most are fatal and incurable. This type of disease can be caused by any of the three agents: bacteria, fungi, or viruses. *Foliar* diseases can also be caused by all three agents. Some are primarily cosmetic and don't do a great deal of harm; others are quite serious and defoliate trees and reduce fruit production. Some symptoms that display first on foliage are not foliar diseases at all, but are indicative of another disorder, or a nutrient deficiency. Root and crown rots are typically caused by fungi. Some of the most common and significant diseases of fruit trees are described in this section. Planting resistant cultivars is often the best way to combat these diseases. See the tables at the end of the chapter for more information about their control and prevention. Not every disease described is prevalent everywhere; contact regional sources, like Agricultural Extension or Master Gardeners for pertinent, local information about fruit tree diseases.

Above and below: Fire blight, shown here, is most effectively addressed by pruning with sterile instruments and carefully disposing of infected parts.

Fire blight is named for the blackened twigs, with dried shriveled leaves still attached, it leaves behind. Afflicted branches look scorched, as if by a blowtorch. Caused by a bacteria, it enters trees through open blossoms and new shoots, killing twigs and branches from the terminal end back toward the trunk. Fire blight attacks fruit trees in the Rose plant family: apple, pear, quince, and loquat. Rainy springs spread fire blight more quickly. Avoid planting highly susceptible varieties to minimize damage. Less-vulnerable varieties are available for apples, including many heirloom cultivars. For pears, the variety Seckel is somewhat less susceptible.

Fire blight infections can severely disfigure or kill fruit trees. Pruning out infected limbs to avert the disease's spread into larger wood is the most common treatment for fire blight. Pruning tool blades must be sterilized before *every* cut. Dip the head of shears into a 10 percent solution of bleach and water between every cut to avoid spreading the bacteria into healthy wood. Bag all cuttings in plastic, as they are cut.

Unless compost pile temperatures of 150°F to 160°F (66°C to 71°C) for three to four days are guaranteed, *do not* put fire blight–infected stems in the compost pile. Cut 18 inches (46 cm) into good wood—that means cut infected branches a foot and a half below visible symptoms. This infection spreads underneath bark, and inhabits wood that looks healthy before symptoms start to show. Bleach water corrodes metal, so thoroughly dry and oil pruning tools after completing fire blight pruning.

Apple scab and pear scab are fungal diseases that infect new leaves and fruit with dark scabby patches that grow together to form large brown lesions. Scab can cause ruined, immature fruit to drop from the tree. Wet springs provide conditions ripe for scab. Orchard cleanup at the end of the growing season is essential to reduce the numbers of overwintering spores in the orchard. Dry springs, and irrigation that keeps tree foliage dry, significantly reduces incidence of scab diseases. Resistant varieties of both apple and pear are available.

Peach leaf curl is a fungal disease that affects both peaches and nectarines. Spores are primarily spread by rain. Attacking foliage first, fruit production of severely infected trees is reduced by this disease. Shortly after blooming is finished, leaves thicken and pucker with red blisters. By late spring, infected leaves turn reddish brown and fall off the tree. Trees will put out a second set of leaves, which will grow

normally if the weather dries up. The energy spent in replacing leaves lost to peach leaf curl will reduce fruit set. Tips of new shoots can also be distorted by this disease. Repeated, severe infections weaken trees. A few varieties of both peach and nectarine have some resistance. Pruning affected shoots does not provide any control. Organic fungicidal sprays applied at the end of the growing season reduce the numbers of overwintering spores and help to control this disease the next spring.

Powdery mildew, another fungal disease of foliage, assaults many different species of plants and trees. Powdery mildew forms a gray-white fuzz over leaf surfaces, and sometimes on flowers, fruits, and shoots as well. Persistent infections can cause leaves to die and drop off. This reduces the tree's capacity for photosynthesis and uses its energy to grow new leaves. Powdery mildew spores need moisture to begin an infection, but get along in dry weather quite well once established. Prevention is the best control

Above right: Peach leaf curl is unsightly and can reduce fruit production. Severely infected leaves may be removed by hand and disposed of (not composted).

Below left: Apple scab on a leaf and fruit. Keep foliage dry during watering and remove highly infected twigs for control.

strategy. Fruit trees need to be planted in full sun and have good air circulation through their canopies. Keep foliage dry, but in arid climates, wash it off occasionally—once or twice during the summer, to remove powdery mildew spores. Use a hose-end nozzle and choose the morning of a clear, dry, warm day. Hose off upper and lower leaf surfaces with a fine, strong spray. Powdery mildew does not flourish on leaf litter; it only infects live foliage. Overwintering spores clinging to bark can be reduced with organic fungicidal sprays applied at the end of the growing season.

Above: Powdery mildew typically shows up on leaves, but can also be found on other parts of a tree.

Right: Organic fungicidal sprays are available on the market or, like dormant oils, can be prepared at home following many online recipes. One effective method calls for 4 teaspoons (18.4 g) baking soda and an equal amount of biodegradable liquid soap mixed with 1 gallon (3.8 L) of water and applied through a spray bottle. Researchers have validated the success of baking soda as a fungicide for many applications, including as a control for powdery mildew.

Brown rot, a fungal disease that spoils fruit, infects all of the stone fruits, including cherries. A full-blown infection can wipe out an entire crop just before harvest. Blooms and new shoots coated with moisture for a minimum of five hours can be infected by spores that overwintered on last year's mummies. Infected blossoms shrivel and do not set fruit. They also harbor spores that will infect fruit later in the growing season. Brown rot on fruit begins as soft brown spots that mushroom into ugly, powdery masses of spores. The fruit is consumed very quickly, but the majority stays attached to the tree. The wrinkled, dried-out mummies cling to their twigs, carrying next year's brown rot spores. Orchard cleanup is the first line of defense against brown rot. Remove or bury *deeply* all mummies on fruit trees and the orchard floor during the end of the season cleanup (do not compost). Abandoned or neglected stone fruit trees near the orchard can also be a source of brown rot spores. Wounds in fruit surfaces made by insects and birds open entry points for brown rot infection. Harvested fruit can also succumb to brown rot. Keep the harvest in cool storage, around 32°F (0°C). Remove any infected fruit right away.

Root and crown rots begin in the soil—usually poorly draining, overly wet soil that crowds out oxygen and stresses tree roots. Trees planted too deeply are especially vulnerable. The organisms that cause these rots are fungi, for the most part, and native to the soils they inhabit. In other words, they're everywhere, all the time. Avoid creating the chronically wet, warm environments that favor their dominance over other micro-flora and fauna living in the root zone.

Initial Symptoms of Rots

Initial symptoms of root and crown rots look like drought stress (causing us to water more!), because roots are dying and failing to deliver water to top growth. Leaves turn yellow, wilt, and fall off. Decline and death of the tree can

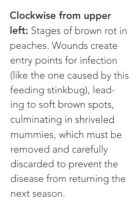

Clockwise from upper left: Stages of brown rot in peaches. Wounds create entry points for infection (like the one caused by this feeding stinkbug), leading to soft brown spots, culminating in shriveled mummies, which must be removed and carefully discarded to prevent the disease from returning the next season.

take years, or only a single season, depending on the type of fungus and where the infection begins. Rotting roots cause trees to linger for a longer period than rots that start at the root crown or basal flare. Treating root and crown rots is difficult and generally futile once disease has become established in the tree. Once root rots make it to the root crown from the periphery, the fate of the tree is sealed.

Prevention is the cure. Practice a deep, infrequent irrigation regime. Keep mulch away from root crowns and basal flares. Plant new trees a little "high" in slower draining soils. Do not irrigate tree trunks; keep basal flares and lower trunks dry. Do not bury the graft union. Do not grow turf grass up to the base of fruit trees.

The genus *Phytophthora* was previously classified as a fungus and is now an *Oomycetes*. Biological classification aside, *Phytophthora* is a significant cause of root rots for subtropical fruit trees. The spores can survive for years in soils that remain moist. Be wary of replanting on old avocado or citrus orchard sites if their soils have not been *completely* dry for at least several months. Both avocado and citrus trees are vulnerable to *Phytophthora* root rots. White sapote trees are resistant.

Verticillium wilt is a vascular disease of plants and trees caused by a soilborne fungus. This organism is distributed in soils worldwide and infects more than 300 different species of trees and plants. Apricot, peach, cherry, and avocado are vulnerable to this disease, although avocado frequently recovers. Apple and pear trees are resistant. Root-knot nematodes can vector verticillium wilt. The fungus enters roots and progresses upward; infected branches die from the bottom up. Verticillium colonizes plant cells and plugs water conducting tissues. It is not able to move laterally inside plants, but only from one cell to the next, end to end. This disease expression can mean one dead branch, or many, or most of the branches on the tree.

There is no cure, and no viable treatment for verticillium wilt, but sometimes trees spontaneously recover, and don't display symptoms again. Sometimes they do, perhaps years later. Remove dead branches or dead trees with as much of the root system and adjacent soil as possible. Do not use wood chips for mulch or compost tree parts from infected trees. If the disease is detected, do not grow other highly susceptible plants such as tomatoes, potatoes, and strawberries, in the orchard. Do not use infected trees, even recovered ones, for propagation of fruitwood or rootstock. Purchase new trees from reputable nurseries. Maintain healthy trees. Prevent drought stress and avoid excess nitrogen.

Overly wet, poor-draining, or soggy soils can lead to root and crown rots. Mulch was allowed to pile up at the base of this apple tree, which was planted too deep and then overwatered, leading to a fungal infection. Keep mulch a few inches clear of the trunk at all times, keep trunks dry, and water deeply and infrequently to prevent root infections.

ENVIRONMENTAL DISORDERS

Environmental disorders, also called *abiotic* diseases, are not diseases at all. Although their symptoms can mimic common diseases or the damage caused by insects and mites, a biological agent is not the cause. When symptoms, but no signs, are observed, the cause may be abiotic. Environmental disorders can be difficult to discern, and it's very important to know the orchard site, the trees, and their history well. Common environmental disorders are described in this section.

Drought stress starts with an off-color look to leaves, a dull, blue cast, rather than a shiny green. Leaves wilt next. Then leaves will dry and drop off, and blossoms and small fruit will, too. Dieback of wood progresses from twigs to branches to the trunk. Roots are dying as well. Caught early, trees exhibiting symptoms of drought stress recover right away—limp leaves perk up quickly after watering. Foliage too dry for too long may still fall off, and the tree will regrow new leaves to replace them.

The environmental disorder caused by too much water is actually an oxygen deficit. At first, this looks like drought stress. Foliage wilts and drops off. Leaves often turn a pale yellow before wilting and falling, though. Additional symptoms of insufficient oxygen are a thinning canopy, slow growth rate, small leaf size, and *chlorosis*—the yellowing of leaves. Twigs may die back. Roots in chronically wet soil can turn black. The soil may look black and smell like rotten eggs. Root rots can take over oxygen-poor, wet soils, changing this environmental disorder into disease.

Broadleaf evergreen trees, like the subtropical fruits, are the most vulnerable to *frost damage*, but if temperatures become cold enough, deciduous trees can be damaged also. Leaves and shoots turn brown, looking scorched. For some species of trees, frost-damaged leaves turn red or purple (it's not the same as autumn color). The top and outside of the canopy sustains injury from frost first. New growth is especially vulnerable; older leaves and stems are more cold-hardy. Late frosts, those that occur in early spring, can be very damaging to blooms and new fruit. Wait to prune off frost-killed branches until after the last frost of the season. Leave the dead leaves and twigs to protect the live wood below from later frosts. Wait until new growth begins below the frost-killed portion to show where the wood is still alive. Prune to the highest live node.

Above: Waterlogged soils can lead to a yellowing of leaves, called chlorosis. Implementing a less-frequent, deeper watering schedule can help.

Left: Drought-stressed, wilting leaves on a crab-apple tree. Water is the cure.

Sunscald is the name given to bark killed by sun exposure; this injury can be preceded by great temperature swings during the winter. Sunscald spreads vertically and occurs on the south- and southwest-facing section of the trunk. Symptoms show at first as discolored bark, reddish or brown; then, it shrinks, dries, cracks, and lifts away from the wood underneath. Live bark at the edges of the injury will try to close the wound. A rounded ridge may form along the perimeter of the damaged area, but a section of the wood will remain exposed. This type of injury is very attractive to wood borers and other decay organisms. Factors that increase risk of sunscald are drought stress, large pruning wounds or mechanical injury to the trunk, and sudden exposure to direct sunlight following severe pruning. Orchard trees often have their trunks whitewashed to reflect light and heat away and reduce sunscald risk. Proper pruning practices that keep trunks shaded are a better, more organic method of reducing sunscald, but to paint fruit tree trunks use a whitewash designed for the purpose. Organic options are always recommended; however, if using latex paint, be sure to use equal parts paint and water. (*Never* apply full-strength house paint to tree trunks.)

The darkened, frost-damaged branch on this fig tree was pruned once the subsequent new growth offshoots revealed the extent of the damage.

Nutrient deficiencies are perhaps the most commonly misdiagnosed environmental disorder. Symptoms of nitrogen deficiency begin with the oldest leaves turning yellow; new leaves remain their normal shade of green. The disorder progresses with smaller than normal leaves and shoot growth that's too short for the fruit tree type. For deciduous trees, autumn leaf drop occurs earlier than it should. Leaves turn yellow during iron deficiency also, but this time, the youngest leaves yellow. The veins of an iron-deficient leaf remain green; it yellows between them. With continuing and severe iron deficiency, new leaves are almost white. Additional symptoms of this disorder are small leaves, normal length shoots that are too narrow, and twig dieback. An alkaline pH and cold, overly wet soils hamper iron uptake by roots. Other micronutrient deficiencies, particularly in citrus, can look a lot like an iron deficiency.

Early sunscald symptoms in a young fruit tree **(left)**. Proper pruning to keep vulnerable trunks shaded is the preferred method of sunscald protection, though many orchardists apply a whitewash to trunks **(above right)**. When using a whitewash, choose an organic-based mixture.

Interveinal chlorosis, or the yellowing of leaves between veins, is a symptom of iron deficiency and/or other micronutrient deficiencies.

Salt damage to trees and plants can occur from soil salts absorbed by roots (through improper fertilization or salty irrigation water), or by salts in solution splashed on foliage (road deicing or sea spray). Symptoms of root-absorbed salt toxicity are yellow foliage, stunted growth, and older leaves with brown edges and tips. Salt toxicity kills plants and trees. Salt-splashed foliage turns brown, but the injury is confined to the portion of the canopy that got "hit." Damaged leaves die and fall off. Chronic exposure to this type of salt toxicity can cause early leaf drop in the autumn, and slow emergence of new leaves in spring. Salts will accumulate in the soil below the splash zone, too.

Smog damages tree leaves, but not all types of fruit trees are susceptible. Discoloration of leaf surfaces is the symptom of this environmental disorder. Presence of high levels of ozone or sulfur dioxide, or both, cause the most visible damage. Leaf surfaces that look flecked or stippled with tiny brown spots that fade to gray or white is typical of ozone injury. This can look a lot like spider mite damage; check the undersides of leaves for signs of the pest before assuming ozone is the culprit. High levels of sulfur dioxide occur in air pollution generated by coal burning. Foliar injury from sulfur dioxide manifests as interveinal bleaching; leaf tissue between the veins turns white—not yellow as in iron deficiency. There's no cure for smog and no treatment for the damage it does to trees.

Trying to grow fruit trees in the urban haze? Choose fruit tree types that are least likely to show damage. Mulberry, avocado, and peach are reportedly vulnerable to ozone. Pears and apricots have a reputation for being resistant.[37]

[37] Griffiths, H. 2003. "Air Pollution on Agricultural Crops." Ontario Ministry of Agriculture: Order No. 85-002.

ANIMAL EXCLUSION

Young trees planted in areas with free-roaming deer or farmed animal populations require protection from browsing until they become established enough to withstand such pressures on their own. Deer are particularly notorious for enjoying a mouthful or ten of nubile fruit tree leaves and for rubbing jagged antlers against fragile trunks. Luckily there are simple, successful, humane solutions. To this end, FTPF encourages the use of nonlethal animal exclusion methods *only*. Not surprisingly, these are also the most effective for protecting an orchard.

Perimeter Fencing

Fencing is a reliable and long-lasting option to protect trees individually or the entire yard. For farmed animals, heavy fencing is necessary, and is typically installed by professionals. Check with local providers for quotes and be sure to arrange an installation prior to the orchard planting. Remember, it only takes one

afternoon of animal access for tree damage to occur. Choose a fence height based on the jumping and climbing characteristics of the animals at large.

For deer, aim high to account for their impressive leaping ability. A 7½-foot (2.3 m) or taller fence works well. Though most deer can clear even these heights when stressed, especially white-tailed deer, under normal conditions, they won't. FTPF has had success using the polypropylene deer fences discussed herein. These are relatively inexpensive, unobtrusive, and easy to install. Be sure to follow the specific directions from the chosen fence manufacturer, along with these general guidelines, when appropriate.

To protect your orchard with fencing:

1. Measure the perimeter of the orchard with a measuring wheel or another device, keeping far enough away from the orchard's edges to prevent browsers from pushing up against

Trees help remove ozone, a major contributor to smog, from the lower atmosphere—but are also damaged by it, as illustrated in this black cherry leaf. In high-smog areas, choose ozone-damage resistant tree types and plant as many as possible to reduce air pollution for the community.

the fence and tugging on a leaf or branch. Add about 10 percent to the total length when procuring the fence to allow for adjustments, installation mistakes, and future repairs.

2. Next, obtain the fence posts. Metal t-posts are generally easier to drive into the ground than other types that require more elaborate post-hole digging. Give preference to recycled posts for environmental reasons. If using t-posts, preferably with a stability plate at the base, choose lengths that are at least 2 to 3 feet (0.6 to 0.9 m) taller than the height of the fence. Obtain enough posts to place one about every 15 feet (4.6 m), plus several extras for added flexibility in the fence design. For sandy, loose soils, or in areas where the ground freezes, plan on driving each post 3 feet (0.9 m) down for maximum stability. Otherwise, aim for at least 2 feet (0.6 m). Test the soil structure in advance to determine the optimal post length.

Use an A-frame ladder and post hole pounder to drive t-posts, with their pegs facing away from the orchard, at about 15-foot (4.6 m) intervals along the fence perimeter. Have someone hold the post upright during initial placement and stabilize the ladder during pounding. Wear gloves when pounding posts to avoid blisters. For those helping hold posts in place, hands should be kept at least two pounder lengths below the top of the post at all times, and bodies out from underneath the action to avoid potential injury.

3. Large fence rolls can be cumbersome, so work in teams. Start at the post adjacent to where the entry gate will be and unroll the fence, keeping the roll upright and on the outer side of the orchard area. Fasten the fence to the pegged side of each post with at least five evenly distributed zip ties, facing the loose end in toward the orchard. Continue in this fashion, one post interval at a time. Be sure to keep the fence taut. Rolling the fence beyond the next post will encourage sagging. If a section appears loose after the fence has been erected, fold and tie any slack over one of the posts. To deal with a slope or gradient change, drive a post at the point where the slope begins and start a new section of fencing there to adjust the angle.

4. Drape about 6 inches (15.2 cm) of the fence on the ground throughout the entire perimeter, folded outward, away from the orchard. Weigh this flap down with heavy, natural materials such as large rocks, to prevent deer and small animals from nudging their way underneath the fence. This will effectively reduce the height by 6 inches (15.2 cm), but it will more than make up for it by blocking off a major thoroughfare into the orchard.

5. Weave natural materials such as grasses or twigs through the grid of the upper fence as a visual indicator to deer that this is indeed a tall obstacle. Pick a tall gate that fits the needs of the orchard in terms of width. Recycled construction materials depots are great places to find gates and other fencing supplies.

When perimeter fencing is not desired, individual trees may be fenced using the same general principles. Make sure at least one side of the enclosure can easily be opened to allow for tree maintenance. With individual fencing, the perimeter tends to be closer to the trees compared to orchard fencing, therefore a more rigid material, such as metal, is recommended. This will prevent large animals from pushing in and grabbing foliage. Choose small grid openings to exclude smaller animals, such as rabbits, as well.

Basic Materials Checklist for Polypropylene Deer Fence Installation

✓ Fence roll(s)

✓ Gate

✓ Posts (e.g., t-posts at 15-foot [4.6 m] intervals, gate posts)

✓ Post pounder

✓ A-frame ladder

✓ Fasteners (e.g., heavy-duty zip ties, at least five per post)

✓ Measuring device (e.g., measuring wheel)

✓ Work gloves

✓ Team of three installers

Baskets, Netting, and Other Deterrents

Burrowing animals sometimes cause damage to young tree roots, but not frequently. Commercially available **gopher baskets** are easily installed to line the planting hole with an exclusionary wire mesh that does not inhibit root growth. Use only if there is a history of gopher damage at the site; or create your own protector by crisscrossing poultry netting with 1-inch (2.5 cm) openings. Allow the netting to extend all the way to the top of the soil, without protruding, making sure to bend any sharp edges downward to protect bare feet.

Birds also appreciate all of the hard work we do to keep our orchards healthy and thriving. Once fruit trees are full of fruit that's almost ripe, they bring their appetites, and their friends. Allowing these beautiful creatures an opportunity to enjoy some of the harvest can be rewarding. Otherwise, excluding birds or deterring them from eating tree fruit can be accomplished without harming them, using nontoxic methods. As soon as bird damage is visible on ripening fruit, deploy exclusion or deterrence tactics with a prepared plan of action.

A good choice for isolated and small trees, bird exclusion with *netting* presents a physical barrier that keeps birds from reaching the fruit at all.

Large home orchards in deer-prone areas can be humanely protected with exclusionary fencing while the trees become established, such as this 7½-foot (2.3 m) tall polypropylene fence that blends in nicely with the surrounding scenery.

Below: Rodents and rabbits that occasionally enjoy gnawing on tender tree trunks can be kept at bay using wire or plastic mesh, or hardware cloth, with ¼-inch (6 mm) openings. Premade "trunk protectors" are also available. Use an appropriate diameter to avoid girdling the tree. When using rigid protectors, create some distance from the trunk to effectively exclude small animals. Remove once the threat dissipates.

Plastic netting should be ¼-to-½-inch (0.6-to-1.3-cm) mesh. It can be draped right over the tree's canopy, but attaching it to posts set just outside and above the tree has additional advantages. Fruit at the edge of the canopy is protected, and retrieving the netting after harvest for reuse next season is easier. Use three or four wooden posts. Position them in a square or triangular pattern, just past the dripline, and set them so that they stand a little taller than the tree. Drape the netting over the ends of the posts and attach with staples or zip ties.

Deterrents keep birds from settling in fruit trees to eat via visual or auditory distractions. A combination of various deterrents that are changed frequently throughout the harvest season is most effective. *Visual deterrents* include flash tape, compact discs, and pie tins. Light reflects from their surfaces. When breezes move these items hanging in the tree, little flashes of sunlight sparkle around the perimeter of the canopy.

Flash tape is an iridescent ribbon available at garden centers and home improvement stores. Cut strips so that they are not shorter than 12 inches (30.5 cm) after tying them in the tree. Choose the ends of twigs at different places around the edge of the canopy. If the birds become accustomed to the pattern, rearrange the strips. CDs and pie tins work the same way; they reflect sunlight and flash when the air stirs them. Pierce a small hole near one edge and hang with string in various places around the canopy, just like the flash tape. CDs should be positioned with the label side toward the leaves, so the shiny side is facing out. These may also need to be rearranged, if the birds get used to them before all of the fruit is picked.

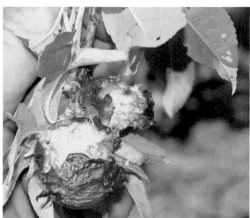

Fruit with typical signs of bird damage

Predator icons deter birds by making them wary. "Scare-eye" balloons or discs can be attached to the edge of the fruit tree canopy. The center of the "eye" is holographic; birds perceive its gaze following them. They will, however, learn that it is harmless, so move this type of deterrent to a new position every few days. Plastic statues of owls and hawks are another version of the predator icon. These must be repositioned at least once a week to remain effective. The predator icon used for centuries, still effective, is the scarecrow, and can be homemade. Just like dummy owls and hawks, scarecrows must be moved to different locations in the orchard regularly. For taller trees, elevating them enhances their effect. (Remember, Dorothy had to help the Scarecrow down from that pole he was hanging on.)

Automatic devices that make a sudden, loud noise at random intervals are also used to deter birds. When combined with visual deterrents, the effectiveness of both devices can be increased and lengthened. A wide variety of these sonic bird deterrents are marketed. Different devices make different types of sounds; some are not audible to the human ear. Remember to turn off sonic bird repellents at night.

Use bird exclusion and deterrents only if there is a risk for significant fruit damage and only for the time they are needed, as the fruit begins to ripen through the end of the harvest. When the harvest season is past, take these devices down and put them away until next year. This helps maintain their effectiveness and helps them last through multiple harvests. Choose reusable barriers and repellents whenever possible. Finally, for success in repelling birds, alternate available food is a factor; well-fed birds are less likely to visit your trees for a snack.

Favorite Fruits for Birds

- ✓ Sweet cherries
- ✓ Mulberries
- ✓ Figs
- ✓ Stone fruits (peaches, nectarines, apricots, etc.)
- ✓ Apples

Fruits Birds Choose Last

- ✓ Citrus
- ✓ Pomegranates (unless ripe fruit has split open)
- ✓ Pears

Common Nonbeneficial Organisms

To provide a basis for identification and remediation, the following table lists common fruit tree types and the organisms and diseases most likely to damage them.

Fruit Type	Insects, Mites, Nematodes	Diseases
Almond	Scale, mites, leafhoppers, leaf rollers, nematodes, borers, Box Elder bug	Root and crown rots, verticillium wilt, bacterial canker, shot hole, brown rot, leafspot
Apple/Pear	Codling moth, plum curculio, apple maggot, aphids, scale, leaf miners, leaf hoppers. Pears only: pear psylla, mealybug, whitefly, thrips, leaf rollers	Fire blight, scab, bacterial canker, root and crown rots, powdery mildew. Pears only: pear decline, rust, leaf spot
Apricot/Cherry	Nematodes, borers, plum curculio, scale, aphids, leaf rollers, other assorted moth caterpillars	Eutypa dieback, root and crown rots, verticillium wilt, bacterial canker, shot hole, brown rot, powdery mildew, crown gall. Cherry only: leaf curl
Avocado	Nematodes, scale, mites, thrips, whitefly, mealybug, leaf rollers	Root and crown rots—esp. Phytophthora, bacterial canker, verticillium wilt
Citrus	Aphids, mealybug, scale (armored and soft), mites, thrips, leaf hoppers, katydids, cutworms, loopers, leaf rollers, tussock moth, snails, whitefly, beetles, nematodes, Asian citrus psyllid	Root and crown rots, bacterial canker, citrus brown rot, leaf spot, Huanglongbing (HLB, citrus greening)
Fig	Mealybug, whitefly, scale, thrips	Root and crown rots
Loquat	Spider mites	Fire blight, scab, leaf spot
Olive	Olive fruit fly, glassy-winged sharpshooter (leaf hopper), scale (armored and soft), borers, nematodes, whitefly	Verticillium wilt, root and crown rots
Peach/Nectarine	Borers, plum curculio, scale, leaf rollers, tent caterpillars, tussock moth	Peach leaf curl, root and crown rots, verticillium wilt, bacterial canker, shot hole, brown rot, powdery mildew, crown gall
Pecan	Aphids	Fungal canker
Persimmon	Borers, nematodes, mealybug, scale, mites, webworms, caterpillars, Fuller rose beetle	Root and crown rots, heart rot, gray mold, leaf spot

Fruit Type	Insects, Mites, Nematodes	Diseases
Plum	Borers, plum curculio, scale, aphids, nematodes, caterpillars, leaf rollers	Peach leaf curl, root and crown rots, verticillium wilt, bacterial canker, shot hole, brown rot, powdery mildew, crown gall
Pomegranate	Mealybug, whitefly	Oak root-rot fungus, botrytis fungus
Quince	Plum curculio, aphids, mealybug, scale (armored and soft), leaf rollers, borers	Fire blight, brown rot, powdery mildew, rust, leaf spot, Nectria canker
Walnut	Nematodes, borers, aphids, mealybug, scale, leaf hoppers, mites, webworms, caterpillars, walnut husk fly, navel orangeworm, codling moth	Root and crown rots, fungal canker, crown gall, anthracnose, walnut blight

Organic, Humane Control Methods (Preferred Applications)

The following table identifies the preferred, most humane control methods available in organic orcharding. For an Earth-friendly outcome, look to these as the first line of defense.

Control Name	What Is Controlled	When to Apply It	How to Apply It	Additional Information
Humane exclusion	Deer, burrowing animals, rodents, birds	Anytime there is a serious threat to tree health	See Animal Exclusion for details.	Fences, nets, trunk protectors, and underground wire baskets prevent animals, small and large, terrestrial or airborne, from damaging fruit trees. Avoid any methods that harm or kill.
Physical removal	Insects (larva or adult), snails, some fungi	Anytime a population is detected	Using hands, hoses, paintbrushes, or other apparatus, gently remove organisms from tree; wash powdery mildew off leaves.	Know the insect or animal's feeding pattern to determine when is the best time to physically remove them from the tree.
Organic horticultural oils (dormant oil, superior oil)	Aphids, caterpillar eggs, leaf hoppers, mealybug, mites, whiteflies, scale, thrips, powdery mildew	Late autumn, after orchard cleanup when trees are dormant and insects are in the egg stage	Spray to branches, trunk and basal flare, including crevices and undersides, until wet.	Low-to-no toxicity to people, noninsect animals and beneficial insects. Works primarily by preventing eggs and spores from developing. Horticultural oils may have a lethal effect on insects if applied when their populations are active. Do not apply in hot, wet, or freezing weather. Do not combine with sulfur fungicides. Not recommended for black walnut.
Organic fungicides (sulfur, copper, sodium bicarbonate)	Scale, thrips, mites, powdery mildew, brown rot, leaf spot, peach leaf curl, rust, scab, fire blight	Late autumn, after orchard cleanup when trees are dormant, 14 to 30 days after applying dormant oil	Mix with water, spray branches, trunk and basal flare, including crevices and undersides, until wet.	Foliage and fruit can be damaged. Use on deciduous trees only. *Do not* use sulfur on apricots. Sulfur can harm beneficial insects. *Do not* apply with horticultural oil. For fire blight, use Bordeaux mix or copper sulfate only.

Control Name	What Is Controlled	When to Apply It	How to Apply It	Additional Information
Kaolin Clay (Surround™)	Apple maggot, plum curculio, codling moth, pear psylla, tent caterpillar, aphids, navel orangeworm, walnut husk fly, thrips, cutworm, leaf hoppers, powdery mildew	Before larvae enter fruit or begin to feed on leaves	Mix with water and spray to coat fruit and foliage.	This method repels the nonbeneficial insects listed. It leaves a white residue on foliage and fruit that can be washed off before eating. May need multiple applications through the growing season.
Beneficial insects	Aphids, psyllids, mites, thrips, caterpillars, whitefly, mealybug	Anytime a population can be maintained	Plantings attractive to beneficials	Attractive plantings that provide habitat for beneficial insects is a more natural, sustainable application of this control method than purchase and release options.
Individual fruit protection (bagging)	Codling moth, stinkbug, cork spot, flyspeck, sooty blotch	When apples or pears are ½ to ¾ inch (1.3 to 1.9 cm) in diameter	See Insects, Mites, and Nematodes for details.	Exclusionary method that reduces fruit defects. Does not affect ripening quality, but will prevent color formation unless fruit is removed several days prior to harvest. Commercially produced bags available or use paper lunch bags.
Organic compost tea	Powdery mildew, botrytis	Before infection	See What Is Compost Tea? for details. Spray on foliage; repeat as needed.	Preventative only. No control of established infections. *E.coli* can live in compost tea. Use organic compost if preparing mixture at home.

Organic, Lethal Control Methods

The following table lists several *less* humane control methods that are common to organic orcharding, so that they may be distinguished from the preferred applications listed in the previous table.

Control Name	What Is Killed	When Applied	How Applied	Additional Information
Organic insecticidal soap	Aphids, psyllids, mites, mealybug, soft scales, earwigs, tent caterpillars, pear slugs	When insects exceed tolerable numbers	Concentrate is mixed with water, or sprayed ready-to-use on foliage, both sides	Used with citrus. Contact with organisms kills them. No residual effect. Repeat applications are usually needed.
Bacillus thuringiensis (Bt)	Most caterpillars, less effective on codling moth and peach tree borer	Timed to match emergence of larvae	Dusted, or mixed with water and sprayed	Applied during late afternoon or on overcast days. Nontoxic to humans.
Organic neem oil	Aphids, thrips, scale whitefly, mealybug, leaf rollers, oriental fruit moth, brown rot, leaf spot, rust, scab, botrytis, shot hole, anthracnose	Early morning or late afternoon to avoid damaging foliage	Mixed with water, sprayed to branches, trunk and basal flare, including crevices and undersides, until wet	Can be mixed with dormant oil. Can irritate eyes and skin. Toxic to bees. Not applied to drought-stressed trees.
Sticky barriers (e.g., Tanglefoot™)	Ants that farm honeydew-producing insects such as aphids and mites	Annually, early spring	Applied on banding material around the trunk, not directly on the bark, according to manufacturer directions	Sticky barriers deter insects from crawling up tree trunks. The lethal effects of such barriers may decrease over time, as insects become aware of their presence and turn away rather than attempt to cross.

Close physical inspection of trees, soil, and surroundings for signs of trouble, on a regular basis, is key to determining appropriate control methods, keeping trees healthy, and enjoying the harvest, discussed next.

chapter eight

ENJOYING THE HARVEST

Harvested tree fruits are still alive after picking. They respire: taking in oxygen and releasing carbon dioxide. Picking tree fruit, like so many other orchard tasks, needs to be done at the right time: not too early, not too late. Unlike some orchard chores, however, plucking the long-awaited harvest of home-grown fruit is a joyous duty.

MATURE FRUIT HAS REACHED ITS FULL size, with skin that may have the characteristic color, but it is not ripe, yet. Ripe fruit is full-size and full-flavored, and should be eaten in short order. Some types of fruit reach their best quality when they are left on the tree until they are ripe. Others should be harvested at optimum maturity, and allowed to ripen off of the tree. Fruit types that should be left to ripen on the tree are nuts, plums, apricots, figs, cherries, Asian pears, and pomegranates. (Pick pomegranates *before* they split open.) Fruits that should be picked at maturity, and ripened off of the tree, include quince, persimmon, European pears, and avocado.

Apples may be picked when ripe or mature. Late-season cultivars are best picked at maturity and ripened off of the tree. Earlier season varieties can be left to ripen on the tree, but be ready to harvest the crop quickly—ripe apples drop from the tree seemingly all at once. Avocado fruits will not ripen on the tree; they must be harvested and ripened. Size is the only visual cue to an avocado fruit's maturity; its skin color doesn't change. Immature avocados will not ripen off of the tree, however. They stay hard with tough, rubbery flesh until they decay. Test avocados for maturity before harvesting the whole crop. After fruits reach full size, pick one or two and see if they ripen within two days to a week or so. If not, wait another week to try the avocado maturity test again.

Ripe citrus fruit "keeps" on the tree. Grapefruits can last for up to eighteen months; lemons tend to drop when the weather heats up. Harvested citrus lasts for about three weeks in the refrigerator. Pick as much as needed, leaving the bulk of the crop on the tree. Gauge ripeness by taste rather than rind color for citrus, but rind color should be deep. The rind should also look a bit stretched, or thin, and a fruit should feel a little heavy for its size.

While harvesting, leave some of the stem attached to each fruit. Tearing the stem out creates an entry point for bacteria, and the fruit will rot sooner. For apples, cherries, and other spur-type fruits, lift fruits until they are upside down, and twist a little. Ripe fruits will come away easily, with stems—and without damaging the spurs left behind to set next season's fruit. Place picked fruits into buckets, baskets, or bags; do not drop them in. Bruises and nicks also create entry points for bacteria. Try not to overfill harvest containers, especially for soft fruits like apricots; fruit on the bottom may be crushed.

Use fruit picking poles for hard-to-reach areas.

Below: Juicing removes fiber and condenses nutrients into a tasty liquid. Citrus juicers utilize a reaming action, while juice extractors mechanically separate pulp from juice. When in doubt about how to make use of excess harvest, reach for the juicer! (And be sure to compost the pulp.)

Pick the whole crop when the time is right. It's best not to leave ripe fruit on the tree (other than citrus); it attracts animals and insects. Pick up fallen fruit, and if it's not good for eating, put it in the compost pile. Put fruit infested with codling moth, plum curculio, and apple maggot in the yard waste can, instead. Cool temperatures slow the respiration of harvested fruits. Pick fruit in the cool of the morning when possible. Placing the harvest in cool storage, about 32°F (0°C), right away helps ensure a long shelf life, too.

Donating a portion or all of the harvest to local food banks and other charitable endeavors is one way to enhance the overall benefit of your orchard and give back to the community. For your family's share, consider juicing, dehydrating, jamming, or using the fruit as ingredients in other dishes to fully enjoy all the culinary possibilities. Many of these options are discussed on page 156, along with recipes from renowned chefs that bridge the gap between the home orchard and kitchen table.

DEHYDRATE YOUR ORCHARD

The only time it is advantageous to let a part of your home orchard go totally dry is when harvested fruit is sitting on a food dehydrator's drying rack. Preparing dried fruit treats is an excellent way to extend the life of the harvest past the growing season and create lightweight, healthy snacks. Best of all, it is simple. Use a dehydrator or follow your favorite sun-drying recipe.

Outdoor drying racks may be fashioned out of untreated stainless steel or plastic screens. Simply place the screen on blocks to increase circulation and prevent fruit from contacting the ground. Place sliced fruits on top, in full sun, covering the rack at night to prevent condensation. As a general rule of thumb, ¼-inch (6 mm) thick slices work well. A second screen can be sandwiched on top to provide protection from curious animals. The National Center for Home

Dehydrated orchard harvest can provide colorful fruit nutrition in the off-season.

Food Preservation recommends a minimum ambient temperature of 86°F (30°C) with humidity under 60 percent, light breezes, and no precipitation for six to twelve days or until fruit is dry and pliable.[38]

For a quicker fix, use a commercial dehydrator inside the home, following specifications for that particular model. Drying time will vary based on the dehydrator's temperature (typically around 130°–140°F, or 54°–60°C), indoor humidity levels, and the size, shape, uniformity, and moisture content of the fruit. Generally speaking, drying times range from six to thirty-six hours for most fruit. Thin slices will fall on the lower end of this range whereas quartered, halved, or whole fruit on the higher.

To prepare fruit for dehydrating:
Wash, pit, and core fruit; remove caps, stems, and seeds. Peel if desired. Cut into uniform slices. Slices that are ¼-inch (6 mm) thick work well for crispier snacks, or cut fruit into quarters or halves for more volume. Fruits commonly halved include apricots, cherries, figs, and plums; sliced fruits include apples, pears, persimmons, and mangos. If desired, dip or spray with fresh lemon juice prior to drying to prevent discoloration from oxidation. For best results, place unpeeled fruit pieces with skin sides down.

Test fruit periodically for pliability to determine readiness. Dry to a consistency that pleases your palate. Cherries are delicious when raisin-like and citrus when brittle. Dry more thoroughly for long-term storage. Experiment with different spices and marinades for a personal touch, keeping in mind that the latter will add moisture and extend drying times. When drying is complete, allow for cooling before transferring into airtight containers. Store in a cool, dark place. Oven drying is also possible; however, it may take twice as long, or longer, while consuming significant energy resources.

---

[38] University of Georgia Cooperative Extension Service. "Preserving Food: Drying Fruits and Vegetables." Published online.

PRESERVING YOUR HARVEST THROUGH CANNING

The canning process, originating in the early 1800s, is commonly used today for the long-term storage of foods—and is particularly effective for fruit jams and jellies. Detailed instructions are readily available, including the U.S. Department of Agriculture's "Complete Guide to Home Canning" series (online). Be sure to follow the specific directions provided by these more comprehensive manuals to ensure optimum food safety and quality before attempting. The following general guidelines offer an introduction only about where to start and what to expect.

Materials: Essential equipment includes glass canning jars (e.g., Mason jars), lids, bands, and a "boiling water canner," also known as a "water bath canner," recommended for high-acid foods such as fruit jams (often available at neighborhood hardware stores).

A deep, covered pot with a removable rack may be substituted for a boiling water canner, as long as there is enough room for 1" to 2" (2.5–5 cm) of boiling water above the jars when fully immersed.

General Instructions

1. Wash jars, lids, and bands thoroughly with soap in hot water. Dry the bands.

2. Heat the jars and lids (not the bands) in hot (not boiling) water. This will prevent breakage when hot foods are added to the glass jars.

3. Prepare the boiling water canner or its substitute by filling it halfway with water, covering, and bringing to a simmer.

4. Remove the jars and lids from the hot water and fill with a jam made according to a favorite recipe (see Jamming with Chef Tal Ronnen section for ideas). Leave about ¼" to ½" (0.5 mm–1 cm) of empty space at the top of the jar

Jams, jellies, preserves, conserves, and marmalades made from orchard fruits can be stored and enjoyed year-round. What differentiates them? Each has its own unique consistency, including mashed fruit (jam), fruit juice (jelly), whole fruit pieces (preserves), a mixture of different jams (conserves), and small pieces of fruit or citrus rind suspended in a jelly (marmalade).

to allow for proper sealing. Remove any air bubbles trapped in the jam mixture with a clean, non-metal utensil.

5. Clean the rim and sides of the jar before centering the lid on top. Screw the band on until tight.

6. Place the filled jars in the boiling water canner or its substitute using a removable rack. Make sure water is able to circulate freely around each of the jars, with 1 to 2 inches (2.5 to 5 cm) of water on top. Add hot water to the canner if needed. Cover the device.

7. Bring from a simmer to a boil. Start to calculate processing time once water is rolling. Boil for a length of time according to the device's or tested recipe's instructions. In general, a quart- or pint-sized jar filled with fruit jams or jellies should be processed for approximately 10 minutes. [39]

8. Adjust the processing time for higher altitudes by adding 1 minute for each 1,000 ft. (305 m) of altitude above sea level (for recipes with less than 20 minutes of processing at sea level). Add 2 minutes for each 1,000 ft. (305 m) of altitude above sea level for recipes that call for more than 20 minutes processing time. [40] Once finished, turn heat off, remove the canner's lid, and allow jars to cool for 5 minutes.

9. Carefully remove the rack or jars from the canner. Never turn jars upside down. Place jars on a towel (in case of breakage), in a safe area, and leave undisturbed for 12 to 24 hours. Do not tighten or adjust the bands, which may disturb the seal.

10. After 12 to 24 hours have passed, test each jar lid for a proper seal through one or all of the following methods:

- Remove the band and lightly pull up on the edge of the lid, which should remain firmly in place.

- Look at the lid for visible downward curvature towards the jar's contents—an indicator of a proper seal.

- Press on the center of the lid, which should not flex much in any direction, up or down.

11. If a jar is not properly sealed within 24 hours, reprocess the contents immediately with a new lid. Once sealed, store the jar in a cool, dark place.

[39] Roberts, T (Virginia Cooperative Extension, Virginia Tech). 2009. Boiling Water Bath Canning. Publication 348-594.

[40] Kendall, P (Colorado State University Extension). 2010. High Altitude Food Preparation Guide. No. P41.

Jamming with Chef Tal Ronnen

Chef Tal Ronnen is one of the most celebrated vegan chefs working today. In the spring of 2008, he became known nationwide as the chef who prepared vegan meals for Oprah Winfrey's 21-day vegan cleanse. He has since catapulted to fame, catering Ellen DeGeneres and Portia de Rossi's vegan wedding, Arianna Huffington's party at the Democratic National Convention, and the first vegan dinner at the U.S. Senate. A graduate of the Natural Gourmet Institute, Chef Tal has worked at the top vegan restaurants in the United States, including Sublime in Fort Lauderdale, Madeleine Bistro in Los Angeles, and Candle 79 in New York City. Additionally, Chef Tal conducts master vegetarian workshops for students and staff at Le Cordon Bleu College campuses nationwide. Chef Tal offered FTPF the following *exclusive* recipes for home orchard fruit jams using peaches, nectarines, plums, or apricots.

Ingredients

6 pounds (2.7 kg) fresh peaches (equivalent to 4 pounds/3 quarts/12 cups when sliced and pitted)

¾ cup (255 g) light agave nectar

½ cup (120 ml) champagne vinegar

¼ to ½ teaspoon salt (to taste)

2 tablespoons (40 g) pectin (note that there will be variations in the pectin instructions and amounts based on what type of pectin is used; check labels accordingly)

Approx. ½ cup (20 g) packed fresh basil leaves or 1 large sprig

1. Blanch and peel the peaches.
2. Remove the pits and place peaches in a food processor to roughly chop (you should have approximately 8 cups [1.9 kg] of puréed fruit).
3. Place fruit in a large, uncovered non-reactive pot.
4. Bring to a simmer and add the agave, vinegar, and salt to taste.
5. Let simmer on medium heat for about 5 minutes.
6. Add the whole basil leaves and let infuse for about another 5 minutes before removing the basil.
7. Make a slurry with the pectin and some of the hot jam until smooth and then add it back to the pot.
8. Cook for about 5 minutes longer at a gentle simmer to activate the pectin.
9. Pour into sterilized jars and follow your favorite recipe for canning jams. (See Preserving Your Harvest Through Canning on page 155.)

Makes 7 cups (2.2 kg) jam
Prep time: 30 minutes

For other jam flavors, substitute the following ingredients for the fruit, spice, and acid, respectively:

Nectarine, ginger (lemon)
Plum, bay leaf, black pepper (red wine vinegar)
Apricot, orange, saffron (white wine vinegar)

Assorted Fruits: Seasonal Fruit in Papillote by Chef Tal

This is one of the simplest desserts to make, and it's a brilliant way to showcase whatever's in season. You just toss ripe fruit with a few herbs and spices, sprinkle on some sweetener, add a pat of nondairy butter, and bake in parchment paper for a few minutes. Papillotes can be made as individual dessert pockets or larger, to share family-style at the table. You can use your imagination in choosing which flavors to put together. There really aren't any rules, but here are a few no-fail combinations.

- Raspberries and mango slices with fresh ginger and mint
- Nectarines and peaches with fresh basil and cinnamon
- Pitted cherries and apricots with vanilla bean and balsamic vinegar
- Blueberries and peaches with lemon zest, fresh thyme, and mint
- Figs and pears with lemon zest, vanilla bean, and balsamic vinegar
- Apples, pears, and dates with cinnamon, nutmeg, cloves, and ginger
- Pears and quince with black pepper and red wine vinegar
- Bananas, kiwis, and pineapple with ginger, star anise, and vanilla bean
- Persimmons and grapes with lemon zest and cinnamon

Ingredients for Each Single-Serving Papillote

Parchment paper

1 tablespoon (14 g) non-hydrogenated vegan margarine such as Earth Balance

1½ cups (250 g) pitted, peeled, and sliced (if necessary) fruit

Pinch of sea salt

1 teaspoon freshly squeezed lemon juice or vinegar

Spices (optional)

1 to 2 tablespoons (20 to 40 g) sweetener such as brown sugar, maple syrup, light or amber agave nectar, cane sugar, honey (if you use it), or raw sugar

1 sprig fresh herb, or more to taste

To serve: your favorite vegan whipped topping

1. Preheat the oven to 450°F (230°C, or gas mark 8). For each single-serving papillote, cut a piece of parchment paper 10 inches (25.4 cm) square, fold it in half, and trim it into a wide semicircle, cutting close to the cut edges of the paper. Unfold the parchment and place the margarine in the center next to the fold.

2. In a medium bowl, combine the fruit, salt, lemon juice, spices (if using), and sweetener and toss to combine.

3. Pile the fruit on top of and around the margarine, keeping near the center of the parchment. Scrape the bowl well to get all the spices and sweetener onto the fruit. Lay the herb sprig (if using) on top.

4. Fold the parchment over the fruit and seal the edges: Starting at one end, fold a small section ¼ inch (6 mm) in toward the center, fold over again, and crease well; continue to fold and crease the edges until the whole parchment is sealed with a firm, final crease at the other end. Place on a baking sheet and bake in the upper third of the oven for 7 minutes.

5. Using a large spatula, transfer the papillote to a serving plate, and cut the parchment open in the center, being careful to stay clear of the steam—it's hot!

6. Dollop a little vegan whipped topping in the center, and place a heaping spoonful on the side for dipping. Serve immediately, and if you've used whole spices, warn your guests that they are not to be eaten.

Makes 1 single-serving papillote
Prep time: 30 minutes (for 4 papillotes)

Apples and Cashews: Celery Root Soup with Granny Smith Apples by Chef Tal

This is the most popular soup I make—people go crazy for it. Throwing in some diced apples at the end adds a surprise tartness, and dots of chive oil give it a sleek, dramatic finish.

Ingredients

Sea salt

3 tablespoons (45 ml) extra-virgin olive oil

2 medium celery roots, peeled and cut into 1-inch (2.5 cm) cubes

2 stalks celery, chopped

1 large onion, chopped

2 quarts (1.9 L) faux chicken or vegetable stock

1 bay leaf

1 cup (260 g) thick Cashew Cream (recipe follows)

Freshly ground black pepper

1 Granny Smith apple, unpeeled, very finely diced

Chive Oil (recipe follows)

1. Place a large stockpot over medium heat. Sprinkle the bottom with a pinch of salt and heat for 1 minute. Add the oil and heat for 30 seconds, being careful not to let it smoke. This will create a nonstick effect.

2. Add the celery root, celery, and onion and sauté for 6 to 10 minutes, stirring often, until soft but not brown. Add the stock and bay leaf, bring to a boil, then reduce the heat and simmer for 30 minutes. Add the Cashew Cream and simmer for an additional 10 minutes.

3. Working in batches, pour the soup into a blender, cover the lid with a towel (the hot liquid tends to erupt), and blend on high. Season with salt and pepper to taste. Ladle into bowls. Place a spoonful of the diced apple in the center of each serving, drizzle the Chive Oil around the apple, and serve.

Makes 6 servings
Prep time: 1 hour, 10 minutes

Chive Oil

1 small bunch chives

½ cup (120 ml) canola oil

Pinch of sea salt and freshly ground black pepper

Blanch the chives for 30 seconds in boiling water, then drain and chill in an ice bath. Drain, wrap the chives in a towel, and squeeze the moisture out. Place in a blender with the remaining ingredients and blend for 2 minutes. Strain through a fine-mesh sieve. Put the chive oil in a plastic squeeze bottle with a small opening or use a spoon for drizzling it on the soup.

Makes ½ cup (120 ml)

Cashew Cream

2 cups (290 g) whole raw cashews (not pieces, which are often dry), rinsed very well under cold water

1. Put the cashews in a bowl and add cold water to cover them. Cover the bowl and refrigerate overnight.

2. Drain the cashews and rinse under cold water. Place them in a blender with enough fresh cold water to cover them by 1 inch (2.5 cm). Blend on high for several minutes until very smooth. (If you're not using a professional high-speed blender such as a Vitamix, which creates an ultra-smooth cream, strain the cashew cream through a fine-mesh sieve.)

To make thick cashew cream, simply reduce the amount of water when they are placed in the blender, so that the water just slightly covers the cashews.

Makes about 2¼ cups thick cream or 3½ cups regular cream, or 585 g
Prep time: 10 minutes, plus soaking overnight

Avocados and Lemons: Summer Chopped Salad by Chef Tal

This is supereasy—a foolproof recipe—but you should make it right before you serve it. Chopped salads can get soggy if they sit around. Kids go crazy for this because of all the great flavors and textures.

Ingredients

¼ pound (113 g) green beans, cut into 1-inch (2.5-cm) pieces

5 radishes, finely diced

Agave nectar

¼ English cucumber, finely diced

12 red and yellow cherry tomatoes, quartered

Kernels from 2 ears raw sweet corn

1 avocado, diced

1 cup (30 g) baby arugula

1 shallot, minced

1 teaspoon minced fresh basil

1 teaspoon minced fresh oregano

Vinaigrette (recipe follows)

1 teaspoon freshly squeezed lemon juice

1. Blanch the green beans in boiling water for 30 seconds, then chill in an ice bath. In the same boiling water, blanch the radishes for 20 seconds, then chill in an ice bath sweetened with a touch of agave nectar.

2. Place all of the ingredients except for the Vinaigrette and lemon juice in a large bowl. Drizzle with the Vinaigrette and toss to coat. Sprinkle the lemon juice on top just before serving.

Makes 4 servings
Prep time: 20 minutes

Vinaigrette

1 tablespoon (15 ml) white wine vinegar

½ teaspoon agave nectar

3 tablespoons (45 ml) extra-virgin olive oil

Sea salt and freshly ground black pepper

Place the vinegar and agave nectar in a small bowl, then, whisking constantly, slowly pour in the oil in a thin stream. Season with salt and pepper to taste.

Grapefruits: Shiso Bites by Chef Tal

These are so easy—a 10-minute recipe but really refreshing and striking on the plate. Shiso is a Japanese leaf with a peppery, minty flavor. The ingredients inside—cayenne and citrus—have a sort of zing to them, and you just fold the leaf in half like a little roll-up and pop it in your mouth.

Ingredients

6 fresh shiso leaves

¼ cup (30 g) peeled and julienned fresh daikon

½ cup (45 g) finely shredded napa cabbage

6 grapefruit segments

1 tablespoon (15 ml) extra-virgin olive oil

Sea salt

Ground cayenne

Black and white sesame seeds

1. Place each shiso leaf on a separate salad plate and divide the daikon and cabbage among them, then top each with a grapefruit segment.

2. Drizzle with the oil and season with salt and cayenne. Sprinkle with the sesame seeds. Serve them flat, but eat them rolled up like a taco.

Makes 6 servings
Prep time: 10 minutes

Apples and Dates: Raspberry Applesauce
by Diana Stobo

Diana Stobo is a classically trained culinary artist, raw food recipe book author, and raw food educator. She uses this expertise as well as her own life-changing experiences to instruct and motivate others to eat for health, vibrance, and beauty. In her award-winning book, *Get Naked Fast! A Guide to Stripping Away the Foods that Weigh You Down*, Diana explains how she became an expert of her own body. Once weighing 247 pounds (112 kg), plagued with disease, Diana dedicates her life now to motivating and inspiring others. As a trained culinary artist, Diana brings a sensational flare to the raw food movement, making easy, delicious, and accessible foods that can heal your body without overwhelming your life! Diana has contributed this set of incredible dessert recipes to provide creative ideas on how to get the most out of your orchard harvest.

Ingredients

   1 apple, cored, peeled, and chopped

   1 pint (340 g) raspberries

   2 Medjool dates, pitted

Place all ingredients in processor or blender.
Process until smooth.

Makes 1 or 2 servings
Prep time: 5 minutes

Apples: Caramel Apple Tart by Diana Stobo

This elegant dessert is more than just good looks and taste. Lucuma is a highly nutritious, exotic Peruvian fruit known as the "Gold of the Incas."

Ingredients

1 green apple, cored

1 tablespoon (7 g) lucuma powder

1 tablespoon (15 ml) pure maple syrup

3 to 5 raw pecan halves, grated

1. Thinly slice or dice the apple.

2. In a medium bowl, mix together lucuma powder and maple syrup until a creamy caramel sauce is made. Add the sliced apple to the caramel sauce and toss to coat.

3. Spoon apple mixture into a small dessert dish, or tart mold, and press down gently. Grate pecans with a cheese grater directly over the apples for a crusted topping. If using a tart mold to make freestanding tarts, gently remove before serving.

Makes 1 tart
Prep time: 5 minutes

Apricots and Cherries: Cherry Apricot Crisp by Diana Stobo

Prepare in a tart mold for an elegant-looking dessert.

Ingredients

1 cup (155 g) fresh cherries, pitted and sliced

2 apricots (seeded and thinly sliced)

¼ teaspoon cinnamon

½ teaspoon agave

Toss sliced cherries and apricots, cinnamon, and agave together in a bowl and let sit to infuse flavors while preparing the topping.

Crisp Ingredients

¼ cup (100 g) raw pecans

1 Medjool date, pitted and chopped

⅛ teaspoon cinnamon

⅛ teaspoon vanilla powder

⅛ teaspoon sea salt

1. Place all ingredients in a processor fitted with an S blade. Pulse until pecans and dates are broken down.

2. Place sliced cherries and apricots in serving dish of choice. Crumble pecan–date mixture on top of cherries and apricots, then press lightly to form a crusty top. Enjoy as is or serve with your favorite nondairy frozen dessert.

Makes 1 or 2 servings
Prep time: 10 minutes

Peaches: Summer Peach Cobbler by Diana Stobo

It's beautiful, sweet, and light. Nothing is more delicious than tree ripened peaches—add a pinch of spice and some crunch and you have the most refreshing dessert.

Ingredients

1 fresh summer peach, halved and sliced thinly

½ teaspoon agave

¼ teaspoon cinnamon

Mix together in bowl and set aside to let juices fuse.

Cobbler Ingredients

¼ cup (35 g) raw cashews

1 Medjool date, pitted and chopped

¼ teaspoon vanilla powder

Pinch of salt

1. Place cobbler ingredients in processor fitted with an S blade and process until dates and cashew begin to stick together, approximately 1 minute.

2. Place peaches in serving dish, ramekin, or ring mold, laying down the layers of peaches one on top of another. Crumble nut and date mixture on top of peaches, lightly pressing mixture with fingers to form a firm topping. Compress lightly, and serve. If using ring mold, compress mixture down slightly and gently remove ring mold.

Makes 1 or 2 servings

Prep time: 10 minutes

Tangerines: Creamy Tangerine-tini by Diana Stobo

This little treat tastes a bit like a "creamsicle." With vibrant citrus and a smooth, creamy texture, it's sure to with the hearts of everyone. Don't forget to serve it in a "pretty" glass.

Ingredients

1 cup (235 ml) almond milk

1 cup (235 ml) tangerine juice, freshly squeezed

1 teaspoon vanilla

2 teaspoons (13 g) agave nectar

½ cup (120 ml) ice cubes

Blend on high 30 seconds. Pour into martini glass, and celebrate your orchard!

Makes 2 drinks

Prep time: 5 minutes

chapter nine

BEYOND THE HOME ORCHARD

Earlier, we conjured an image of a place in your yard where family members could sit underneath thriving fruit trees, among the songbirds, clean air, and bountiful harvest overhead. Now, imagine an orchard in a public park or garden where the entire community can do the same, serving as a safe haven for gatherings and educational workshops. Or imagine a schoolyard orchard doubling as an outdoor classroom in which students learn about sustainability while improving school nutrition. Creating community orchards for everyone's benefit can be even more rewarding than a home orchard.

Picture this: a city block lined with fruit trees, where taking a lunch break assumes an entirely new meaning. Public athletic fields adjacent to fruit tree groves where thirsty visitors enjoy nature's perfect thirst-quenchers, without the artificial colors. Envision urban orchards as common as produce stands or supermarkets, minus the cashiers—situated on abandoned lots, community gardens, food bank farms, or through local health centers eager to offer organic harvest to accelerate patient healing.

Through strategic site selection, community orchards provide real solutions to the Earth's most pressing problems, ranging from environmental degradation to nutritional deficiencies. The possibilities are limitless. What better way to make a positive impact in your region than by applying the horticultural principles learned in your home orchard toward a greater good? Community starts with each of us. An orchard is planted one tree at a time.

For general guidance on how to turn community orchard ideas into actual orchards, we offer the following framework, based on FTPF's experience with hundreds of unique planting projects.

COMMUNITY ORCHARD COMMITTEE

Successful planting projects start with a core group dedicated to coordinating and caring for the orchard over time. Approach local community leaders, dignitaries, gardening associations, agricultural extension offices, school principals, health clinics, nature centers, food banks, homeless shelters, drug rehabs, or whoever might share your vision for an orchard. Recruit interested participants to join a volunteer community orchard planning committee to guide the project.

Above: Rescued farmed animal sanctuaries make wonderful locations for orchard projects. Anyone who has seen a goat and an apple in close proximity to each another knows that the apple doesn't stand a chance, as illustrated here.

"All these trees we're planting remind me of hope."

—Jeff Greene, community gardener, during an FTPF orchard project to benefit San Francisco's homeless community (as reported in the *San Francisco Chronicle*)

Become familiar with the published research on the benefits of community orchards in order to drum up support. For example, the University of Georgia Forest Resources Unit reports that community trees have a significant positive impact upon water and air quality, noise abatement, animal habitats, property values, economic stability for communities, human social interactions, and reduction of water runoff, soil erosion, and airborne pollution.[42] University of Illinois researchers conclude that the presence of trees in urban green spaces strengthens neighborhoods, fosters a sense of safety and security, and discourages criminal activities.[43] Another study at the university found that for those who lived near nature, such as an area with trees, levels of aggression, violence, and property crime were reduced while optimism when dealing with the hardships of poverty increased—and neighborhoods were friendlier.[44] Compel decision makers to support your project for a safer, healthier, and friendlier neighborhood.

The director of the USDA's Center for Urban Forest Research writes, " ... trees can be the ultimate multi-taskers, cleaning the air while they cool the city, protecting our climate and reducing polluted runoff."[41] This mature paw paw tree in a public park accomplishes all of the above, and then some, by providing nutrition for the community.

[41] McPherson, E.G. 2005 Apr 1. "Trees with Benefits." *American Nurseryman*.

[42] Coder R. D. 1996 Oct. "Identified Benefits of Community Trees and Forests." University of Georgia, Cooperative Extension Service, Forest Resources Unit Publication #FOR96-39.

[43] Kuo F. E., et al. 1998. "Fertile Ground for Community: Inner-City Neighborhood Common Spaces." *American Journal of Community Psychology*. 26: 6, 823–851.

[44] Human-Environment Research Laboratory, University of Illinois at Urbana–Champaign. *Cooler in the Shade*. Newsletter Vol. 1 No. 6.

Choose committee members with complementary skill sets. Some may have extensive horticultural and fruit tree care experience while others possess a knack for community outreach. Work together as a group to add members who are eager to contribute time, resources, and expertise. Fruit trees are long-term investments and initial enthusiasm may be high, so partnering with folks who see the bigger picture and are in it for the long haul is the best way to build a solid foundation.

Next, as a committee, *identify local nonprofits or public use areas with green space* that would make excellent candidates for a planting. Consider the topics presented in this handbook to determine the appropriateness of a site. Keep in mind the necessity of a permanent water source in close proximity to the orchard, as well as fencing to protect trees from potential predators such as deer or vandalism, if either is prevalent. Research how many community members a potential orchard recipient serves in order to determine the impact of the project. Approach their management with a formal proposal describing project goals, including a cost estimate for the required elements (at a minimum, trees, mulch, tools, and volunteers). Offer your committee's resources (monetary, labor, tools, or all three) to make the proposal a reality. Most orchard budgets are reasonable, especially if the community bands together to pitch in.

If the potential recipient is genuinely committed to the orchard and grants written permission to plant on its grounds, request a *"buy-in"* element to ensure that all parties have a vested interest. History shows that levels of care and maintenance are elevated when gift-receiving parties also make an investment in the project, as opposed to just receiving a freebie. Buy-ins come in different forms, small and large, including, but not limited to: general funding, covering the cost of a certain project element (e.g., drip irrigation materials, fencing, mulch),

predigging holes, providing labor or volunteer support to maintain the orchard, or assigning development staff to help with fund-raising. Avoid forcing any project through if the potential recipient isn't willing to contribute to the effort.

OUTREACH

Once the project framework is established, outreach to local nurseries and equipment suppliers to request discounted rates or outright donations of materials. Remind them that the effort is by the community *for* the community, and offer to mention their support on all promotional materials. To minimize environmental impact, give preference to local suppliers and always look to use recycled materials first, such as free local sources of wood chips for mulch.

Prior to event day, meet at the site with committee members and an arborist or landscape designer to *design the layout of the orchard* according to the principles discussed in previous chapters. Get a feel for how much installation labor will be needed in order to plan for sufficient volunteers. Test-dig a hole manually to ensure that it is possible to do so and there

are no underground surprises. Ask the recipient to mark any underground obstacles, such as waterlines, that should be avoided. Make sure there will be access to irrigation for the trees, and bathrooms for the volunteers, during the planting.

When scheduling the planting date, keep in mind that weekends typically attract the most volunteers. During particularly hot days, start the event in the cool of the morning or late afternoon. For large projects, consider digging some holes in advance to allow volunteers to focus more on planting, especially if many children are expected to participate.

At a minimum, recruit at least one adult volunteer for every two trees planted. Aim to have more. Invite everyone, including dignitaries, local businesses, associations, and civic leaders. Ask volunteers to bring shovels, bow rakes, pickaxes, wheelbarrows, hoses, or anything else that is needed. With sufficient volunteers, an orchard can be created in just half a day. *An instant orchard!*

Publicize the event by sending a press release to local media several weeks in advance as a call for volunteers, and then again one week prior to urge print and broadcast outlets to cover the planting itself. Be sure to take high-resolution photos at the planting to share with interested media afterward and also to tell the story of the orchard in your own materials. The more folks hear about your collective efforts, the more the message will spread, and the more trees will be planted. Remember, the fruit of the tree is on the limb, so branch out to your community and spread the word—you never know which future orchard it will lead to.

EVENT DAY

Launch the event with an arborist or experienced fruit tree planter demonstrating proper planting techniques to volunteers (follow the

This cluster of *plums* can provide a hydrating treat for at least seven individuals.

instructions in chapter 4, Planting). Remind folks to always be mindful of others when wielding tools and to be gentle with the trees, investing extra time to plant each one carefully, especially with regards to planting depth. Let them know that taking an extra five minutes to get things right at the time of planting can make a difference of decades in that tree's lifetime. When in doubt about any step in the process, volunteers should be encouraged to ask for guidance before completing the task.

Break up into groups of two adults per tree. Children should always be paired with adults and kept as involved as possible—after all, these trees are for their future. Child-size gardening gloves and tools come in handy. Pushing backfill into the hole, spreading mulch, and watering are all great activities for young ones. Creating a permanent sign to commemorate the orchard or individual trees is also a rewarding art project for children.

Assign the most experienced planters to roam the orchard and oversee the work, making sure trees are going into the ground correctly. Ask volunteers to check with roamers when unsure

about any aspect of the planting. Instructions on root pruning, planting depth, or tree orientation can be difficult to grasp at first or hard to remember while working in the field. If incorrect, don't be afraid to redo the task. Now is the time to make it right, before the tree becomes established.

Post a sign-in sheet to collect contact information for volunteers in order to provide them with orchard updates and urge them to sign up for maintenance tasks. Immediately after the event, designate specific roles and maintenance schedules for the recipient's staff and orchard committee members; include tasks such as watering, mulching, weeding, fertilizing, pruning, and troubleshooting. When working with students, in order to build orchard pride, ask teachers to assign small groups to care for individual trees throughout the school year.

Everyone benefits from community tree plantings. So make it a party to celebrate the greening of the neighborhood. Bring food, play music, dance, exchange stories, get your hands dirty all together. Most important, invite the young ones. Remind them that these trees will take root for decades and can nourish them, their children, and their children's children. Encourage youth to transcend the event itself by applying the environmental principles learned to their everyday lives. There is no greater outcome than inspiring future generations to get busy making positive change. Encourage all volunteers to plant more trees, whether at home or elsewhere.

Anywhere fruit trees are planted, there are profound benefits. Some call it magic. We hope this handbook has provided the tools needed to spread that magic to your home orchard and beyond. May your trees be abundantly fruitful and your efforts to green the community ripe with success; and may all of us collectively serve as agents of progress for the environment and future generations, one orchard at a time.

Children enjoy helping water newly planted fruit trees.

COMMUNITY ORCHARD PLANTING CHECKLIST

✓ Form a volunteer community orchard committee

✓ Identify local nonprofits or public spaces where an orchard would thrive

✓ Approach decision makers with a proposal and budget estimate

✓ Secure written permission to plant and "buy-in" from recipient

✓ Design orchard layout to determine all the needs

✓ Outreach to local nurseries, businesses, and organizations for support

✓ Procure plant materials, mulch, tools, and if necessary, irrigation and fencing supplies

✓ Publicize the planting with local media outlets and put a call out for volunteers

✓ Predig holes if appropriate

✓ Plant the orchard on event day

✓ Assign maintenance tasks to orchard caretakers

✓ Repeat at another worthy site

Above and left: Typical scenes from FTPF community orchard plantings include smiles on the faces of children, birds perching on newly planted trees, elders crying tears of joy, contented high fives and handshakes through globs of soil stuck to fingers, and mini-rainbows as sunlight shines through irrigation spray onto newly planted root-balls.

COMMUNITY ORCHARDS SPEAK VOLUMES!

Community orchards have far-reaching effects, beyond even the site boundaries themselves. Visitors instantly grasp the intent of the project and often take the idea home with them, as word of mouth and media reports spread the message even further. Orchards serve as inspiration, as models for others to emulate.

In India, FTPF planted thousands of trees at numerous events with low-income schools, each of which was highly publicized in local newspapers and through colorful village parades where schoolchildren announced that "trees are good, plant them!" Government officials took note, inviting FTPF and its partners to expand the effort. Within weeks, other inspired groups in the region officially launched an entire green movement and thousands of additional trees were planted.

Working with students in Brazil, a local mayor heard about the initiative and thanked us " . . . not only for bringing the fruit trees to our town, but also for bringing the seeds of environmental consciousness." Such projects also bring people closer together. In California, an FTPF orchard serving individuals with developmental disabilities "inspired a whole community," according to the director of the facility.

This is the power of a community orchard project.

Indian students working with FTPF let their village know during this parade that the time to plant fruit trees is now!

Contact FTPF

The Fruit Tree Planting Foundation is an international charity serving as a resource to fruit tree planters worldwide. If you have an idea for an orchard that will impact your community, let us know—we may be able to help. If you are already working on a project and are looking for advice, our doors (and phone lines) are always open. If you have planted fruit trees as a result of reading this handbook, please email us the details and photos at **info@ftpf.org**—we will compile the results and publish them. Learn more about FTPF's groundbreaking work at **www.ftpf.org**.

"The Fruit Tree Planting Foundation's groundbreaking work feeds communities in need and greens the environment, all at once. A truly extraordinary, yet simple, concept that led to our collaboration to plant fruit trees in the WE Garden in Capitol Park to help our communities for years to come."
–Maria Shriver, former First Lady of California

"I have a profound reverence for what the Fruit Tree Palnting Foundation does for different cities around the country." –Ariel E. Reboyras, Alderman, City of Chicago, Illinois

"A seed, a sapling, a tree that will feed the body, replenish the Earth, oxygenate the air we breathe for more years than the hands that plant them will live to see. The Fruit Tree Planting Foundation truly embraces the notion that love gives without expectation of reward." –Angela Bassett, Actress

"The Fruit Tree Planting Foundation is single-handedly taking responsibility for the future of our Earth! It is vital and absolutely essential to support this fantastic nonprofit organization!" –Bryce Dallas Howard, Actress

"You're changing the world, one yard at a time." –Ed Begley, Jr., Actor and Activist

GLOSSARY

Abiotic: disease of plants and trees not caused by the activity of a pest or pathogen, but by adverse environmental conditions

Adhesion: molecular attraction between water molecules and molecules of other substances (e.g., soil particles)

Aerobic: natural process occurring in the presence of oxygen

Alternate Bearing: tendency to produce a heavy crop of fruit or nuts one season and a very light crop the next

Amendments: materials added to increase nutrient content or change physical properties of soil

Anaerobic: natural process occurring in the absence of, or not requiring oxygen

Angle of Attachment: angle where a branch and the central leader, or another branch, meet

Annual: a plant that completes its life cycle, seed to seed, in a single growing season

Apical Dominance: the inhibition of lateral buds by dominant terminal buds through the release of hormones

Backfill: soil or potting medium returned to the planting hole

Balled and Burlapped (B&B): field-grown tree, harvested with the root-ball wrapped in burlap or plastic and secured with wire or metal strapping

Bareroot: plants or trees not planted in a container or soil medium, usually dormant, with roots packed in moist sawdust

Basal Flare: trunk section much greater in diameter than the remainder of the trunk, at the root crown

Berm: raised, shaped mound of dirt or rocks, typically constructed to corral or direct water

Branch Bark Ridge: enlarged section of bark tissue on the upper edge of the junction between branches, or between branch and trunk

Branch Collar: area of swollen tissue at the base of a branch

Buttress Roots: large woody roots at the base of the trunk

Canopy: portion of the crown consisting of leaves and twigs, but excluding large limbs

Central Leader: main stem of a tree or sapling (i.e., trunk, bole)

Chill Hours: typically defined as the number of hours at temperatures between 32°F and 45°F (0°C and 7°C); calculated by some to include any temperature below 45°F (7°C)

Chlorosis: yellowing of foliage caused by chlorophyll deficiency

Codominant Stem: stem growing closely adjacent to the trunk or central leader, with a similar diameter and narrow angle in between

Cohesion: molecular attraction between water molecules

Companion Plants: complementary plants that encourage or result in mutualistic relationships with other species

Compartmentalization: process of limiting spread of decay inside trees through chemical and physical boundaries (e.g., in response to a wound)

Conk: fruiting or spore-forming tissue of wood-decaying fungi, found on outside of trunks and branches

Contact Herbicide: a substance that kills plant tissues it touches

Cover Crop: mass planting grown for one season, primarily to provide ground cover or to improve soil properties, rather than a harvestable yield

Cropping: soil nutrient reduction following the removal of crops and plant residues

Cross-Pollination: transfer of pollen from anthers of flowers from one fruit tree cultivar to the stigmas of another fruit tree cultivar

Crotch: the point where two branches, or a branch and the trunk, meet

Crown: total leaves and branches of a tree

Cultivar: selected or bred variety with defining characteristics different from the species

Cultivation: the practice of shallow tilling to uproot weeds

Dripline: outermost edge of a tree's crown

Espalier: pruning system that trains trees to grow against a flat vertical surface (e.g., walls, fences)

Evapotranspiration (ET): the sum of transpiration from plants and trees and evaporation from the soil's surface

Field Capacity: maximum amount of water a soil can hold against the force of gravity

Fruit Thinning: pruning to remove a number of immature fruits to increase size and quality of remaining fruits

Fruitwood: scion; shoot or bud grafted onto rootstock

Genetic Dwarf Fruit Tree: scion bred for dwarfing quality of mature tree independent of rootstock influence

Genus: a group of similar species

Graft Union: area of trunk where the rootstock is joined to a scion

Gravitational Water: water that moves past the root zone under the force of gravity

Green Manure: cover crops tilled under when green to enhance soil structure and fertility

Groundwater Recharge: the return of water to the underground water table

Hardscape: the nonliving, constructed elements of a landscape (e.g., patios, decks, fences, walls)

Heading Cuts: pruning cuts made between nodes

Heeling In: laying a bareroot tree in a shallow trench and covering its roots with soil or moist sawdust for storage until planting

Herbaceous: a plant or plant part that does not form woody tissue

Honeydew: excretion of some sap-sucking insects such as aphids, mealybugs, whiteflies, and soft scales, consisting primarily of water and sugar

Hooks: old lateral branches growing toward the ground in an open-vase form tree

Horticultural Therapy: a therapeutic program of growing plants that has been used for centuries to improve well-being and reduce stress

Included Bark: bark from two stems at their juncture growing inward, typically resulting in a weak connection

Infiltration Rate: the rate at which water can be absorbed by soil

Inorganic: substance not containing carbon; also used to designate fertilizers of a mineral origin

Internodal: relating to the length of stem between nodes

Interstock: a second rootstock, grafted between the first rootstock and the scion

Interveinal: between leaf veins

Latent Buds: buds more than one year old that remain near the surface of the bark

Leaching: removing salts or other soluble materials from the root zone with irrigation and drainage; can lead to nutrient-loss

Living Mulch: a single type of herbaceous plant undersown with a main crop, to serve the functions of a mulch, grown for more than one season

Loam: a soil type containing roughly equal amounts of sand, silt, and clay

Low-Chill: temperate zone fruit tree cultivars that can achieve dormancy with a minimum of chill hours

Microclimate: variations from regional climates under the influence of elevation, slope, exposure, and structures

Modified Central Leader: pruning system that uses heading cuts to the central leader to maintain a designated tree height

Mulch: layer of materials placed on the soil's surface to conserve moisture, reduce weed growth, prevent erosion, moderate soil temperature, and improve aesthetics

Node: point on a stem where leaves are attached

Open-Vase Form: pruning system that heads the central leader to 18 to 36 inches (45.7 to 91.4 cm) and spreads scaffold limbs to nearly horizontal; creates a more open center with multiple leaders in a vaselike pattern

Organic: substance containing carbon and hydrogen atoms; popular term used to designate agriculture and horticulture without the use of synthetic pesticides or fertilizers

Perennial: plants, woody and herbaceous, that live longer than two growing seasons and flower more than once

Perfect (Hermaphroditic): flowers having both male and female organs, capable of self-pollination

Permaculture: holistic agricultural designs that mimic natural ecosystems to maximize harmony between all elements

pH: a numeric scale of 0 to 14 used to describe relative acidity or alkalinity

Photosynthesis: process that transforms CO_2 and water into sugar and oxygen using chlorophyll and light

Pollination: transfer of pollen from flower anthers to stigma

Pollinator: nonplant agents that aid in the spread of pollen (e.g., bees, hummingbirds, wind)

Precipitation Rate: the measure of water dispersal by irrigation systems (e.g., inches per hour, gallons per hour)

Rainwater Harvesting: the gathering and storing of rain to provide water for various purposes, including crop irrigation

Respiration: cellular process that breaks down sugar to release energy; oxygen is consumed, carbon dioxide expelled

Rhizome: a horizontal rooting stem with nodes and buds

Root-Ball: roots and soil of containerized or balled and burlapped plants and trees

Root Crown: place where the root system and the base of the trunk meet

Root Plate: circumference of a tree's large anchoring roots within the top 18 to 24 inches (45.7 to 61 cm) of soil

Rootstock: cultivar or seedling grown to form the root system and base of the trunk for a grafted tree or plant

Root Zone (Rhizosphere): soil surrounding and influencing plant and tree roots, usually the top 18 to 24 inches (45.7 to 61 cm)

Scaffold Limb: a large branch that forms part of the main structure of a tree's canopy

Self-Fruitful: able to produce normal fruit from self-pollinated flowers

Self-Thinning: tendency of trees to drop a portion of immature fruits

Self-Unfruitful (Self-Incompatibility): unable to self-pollinate perfect flowers, cannot set fruit without cross-pollination

Semidwarf Rootstock: rootstock selected to reduce the overall mature height of fruit trees from 50 to 75 percent of standard rootstocks

Sign: evidence of the presence or activity of a pest or pathogen

Soil Drainage: water movement through the soil profile

Soil Pores: open spaces between soil particles

Soil Structure: arrangement of soil particles into larger units (e.g., clods, plates, grains)

Soil Texture: proportions of clay (defined as mineral particles having a diameter of less than 0.002 mm), silt (0.002 to 0.05 mm), and sand (.005 to 2 mm), in a soil;[45] coarseness or fineness of soil

Species: a group of closely related individual organisms that resemble each other and inter-breed freely

Spurs: stubby shoots bearing primarily flowers, productive for multiple growing seasons

Stem-Girdling Root: root closely circling the trunk, constricting trunk growth and that of other roots

Stomata: pores in leaves that exchange gases and let water vapor escape

Suckers: vigorous, upright shoots growing from buds below the graft union

Symptom: change in appearance or growth, or both, of a plant in response to damage by a pest or pathogen

Taper: diameter change in trunks: wider at base, narrower in middle

Terminal Bud: unexpanded growth point at the end of a stem or branch

Thinning Cuts: pruning cuts that remove a branch from the point of origin or at the juncture with another branch

---

[45] Soil Conservation Service, U.S. Department of Agriculture. 1987. "Soil Mechanics Level 1 – Module 3."

Topped (Topping): indiscriminate heading cuts to central leader and scaffold limbs

Transpiration: the loss of water vapor from plant tissues to the atmosphere

True-Dwarfing Rootstock: rootstock selected to result in a mature fruit tree with a height of 5 to 7 feet (1.5 to 2.1 m)

Turgidity: tissue swelling, distended with fluid

Urban Tree (Urban Forest): trees that live within or near populated regions

Variety: naturally occurring variation from a species

Vector: organism capable of carrying and transmitting pathogens to host plants or trees

Vegan: a lifestyle without animal products or practices that contribute to animal suffering

Water Sprouts: vigorous, upright shoots growing from branches or the trunk, above the graft union

Windthrow: failure occurring at the base of the tree, which lifts the root plate out of the soil, usually a result of strong winds

Xeriscape: landscape design philosophy using seven principles to minimize the need for irrigation

RECOMMENDED READING

Composting

Let It Rot!: The Gardener's Guide to Composting. Stu Campbell. Storey Publishing, 1998.

The Rodale Book of Composting: Easy Methods for Every Gardener. Deborah Martin and Grace Gershuny (Editors). Rodale Press, 1992.

Culinary Uses of Fruit

Superfoods: The Food and Medicine of the Future. David Wolfe. North Atlantic Books, 2009.

The Conscious Cook. Tal Ronnen. HarperCollins Publishers, 2009.

Get Naked Fast: A Guide to Stripping Away the Foods that Weigh You Down. Diana Stobo. Bree Noa Publishing Co, 2010.

Fruit Tree Growing

The Home Orchard. Chuck Ingels, Pamela Geisel, and Maxwell Norton. University of California Agriculture and Natural Resources Publication 3485, 2007.

Humane Animal Exclusion Principles

Wild Neighbors: The Humane Approach to Living with Wildlife (2nd Edition). John Hadidian, et al. Humane Society Press, 2007.

Inspirational

The Man Who Planted Trees. Jean Giono. First published in 1953.

Natural Farming and Permaculture

The One-Straw Revolution: An Introduction to Natural Farming. Masanobu Fukuoka, Rodale Press, 1978.

Organic Gardening

Rodale's Ultimate Encyclopedia of Organic Gardening. F. M. Bradley, B. W. Ellis, and E. Phillips. Rodale Press, 2009.

Pruning

Pruning. Susan Lang. Sunset Books, Inc. 1998.

Rainwater Harvesting

Rainwater Harvesting for Drylands (Vol. 1). Brad Lancaster. Rainsource Press, 2006.

Web Resources

The Fruit Tree Planting Foundation: www.ftpf.org

The California Backyard Orchard, University of California: homeorchard.ucdavis.edu

National Sustainable Agriculture Information Service (ATTRA): attra.ncat.org

Trees Are Good, International Society of Arboriculture: www.treesaregood.org

U.S. Department of Agriculture Plant Hardiness Zone Map: www.usna.usda.gov/Hardzone/index.html

U.S. Department of Agriculture Cooperative Extension System Offices: www.csrees.usda.gov/Extension/index.html

INDEX

A

abiotic diseases, 135–138

adhesion, 80

air circulation, 26

air pollution, 14, 16

air purification, 14, 16

alternate bear, 110

anaerobic organisms, 121

anchoring plants, 118

animal exclusion, 139–143

animal manure, 92

annual yield, 18

ants, 125

anvi shears, 100–101, 102

aphids, 124

apple scab, 131

apple trees, 12, 15

apples, 151

automatic deterrent devices, 143

avocado, 151

avocado trees, 48–49

B

bacillus thuringiensis (Bt), 148

backfill, 72

bagging, 147

balled and burlapped (B&B) trees, 56

bareroot trees, 57, 59, 70

bark, 16

basal flare, 41, 42

baskets, 141

bees, 127

beetles, 127

berms, 73

birds, 141ñ143

black sooty mold, 125

bow rake, 63

branch bark ridge, 99

branch collar, 99

branches, 52, 99, 105

brown rot, 132, 133

bypass shears, 100–101

C

calcium, 90

canning, 155–156

canopy, 42

caramel apple tart, 164

carbon dioxide, 14, 26

cashew cream, 160

celery root soup with Granny Smith apples, 159–160

central leader, 52

central leader form, 107, 108

ceramic containers, 38

cherry apricot crisp, 165

chewing insects, 127–128

children, 57

chill hours, 50–51

chive oil, 160

citrus fruit, 151

citrus trees, 97, 108

IMAGE CREDITS

Primary Photographers

Juliana Garske: pages 17 (bottom); 19; 23; 26 (top); 26 (bottom); 29 (top left); 29 (middle left); 30 (top); 31; 38; 39; 43 (top); 43 (middle bottom); 43 (bottom); 47 (left); 47 (right); 53 (cacao fruit); 53 (cacao tree); 53 (pawpaw); 53 (pomegranate); 54 (right); 55 (top); 55 (middle); 55 (bottom); 56; 58; 64 (right); 65 (bottom); 68 (top left); 68 (top right); 68 (middle left); 68 (middle right); 68 (bottom left); 68 (bottom right); 69 (bottom left); 69 (bottom middle); 69 (bottom right); 71 (top right); 71 (bottom right); 72 (top); 72 (bottom); 74 (bottom); 85 (bottom left); 86; 94; 95 (top left); 95 (top middle); 95 (top right); 95 (bottom); 98; 102 (top left); 102 (top right); 103 (left); 104 (bottom left); 104 (bottom right); 105 (bottom); 106 (top left); 109 (top); 109 (bottom left); 109 (bottom right); 116; 121; 122 (top); 123 (bottom); 127 (top left); 127 (top right); 129 (top); 132 (bottom); 134; 135 (left); 149 (bottom right); 150; 151; 152 (left); 152 (right); 153; 155; 168; 170; 173 (top); 174 (bottom); and 192 (top)

Cem Akın: pages 2; 8; 9; 10; 11; 12; 13 (top); 14; 15 (top); 15 (bottom); 16; 17 (top); 20; 25 (top left); 25 (top right); 25 (bottom); 29 (top right); 29 (bottom right); 30 (bottom); 34 (top); 34 (bottom); 35 (top); 35 (bottom); 37; 40; 43 (middle top); 45 (top); 45 (bottom); 46; 48; 49; 50; 53 (fig); 53 (jackfruit); 53 (jujube); 53 (loquat); 53 (olive); 53 (papaya); 53 (persimmon); 53 (tamarind); 54 (left); 57; 60; 61; 63; 64 (left); 65 (top); 66; 67; 69 (top); 73 (top); 73 (bottom); 78; 80 (bottom); 83; 85 (bottom right); 87; 97; 99 (bottom); 101; 104 (top); 105 (top); 106 (top right); 106 (bottom); 118; 119; 120; 123 (top); 129 (bottom); 133 (top left); 133 (top right); 133 (middle right); 133 (bottom left); 133 (bottom right); 136; 140; 141; 142 (left); 169 (bottom); 171; 172; 173 (bottom); and 174 (top)

Illustrator

Ömer Akın: pages 13 (bottom); 21; 24; 32; 41; 44 (top); 59; 75; 76; 77; 79; 80 (top); 99 (top); 102 (bottom); 103 (top right); 103 (bottom right); 107; 108 (bottom left); 108 (bottom center); 108 (bottom right); and 111 (top)

Recipes

Recipes and photos are reprinted with permission from: **The Conscious Cook © 2009 Tal Ronnen and Melcher Media**: pages 158; 159; 161; and 162

Diana Stobo: pages 163; 164; 165; 166; and 167

Contributing Photographers

Agricultural Research Service, USDA: pages 124 (top); 124 (bottom right); 125 (top left); 125 (top right); 125 (middle left); 125 (bottom right); 126 (top right); 126 (middle left); 126 (middle right); 126 (bottom left); 126 (bottom right); and 127 (bottom)

Elias Blood: pages 44 (bottom); 70; 71 (left); 74 (top); 82; 85 (top right); 113; and 115

Jill Ettinger: pages 53 (chestnut); 62; and 137 (left)

Florida Division of Plant Industry Archive, Florida Department of Agriculture and Consumer Services, Bugwood.org: page 128

The Fruit Tree Planting Foundation: pages 5 and 175

Nancy Gutknecht: page 22

Will Hudson, University of Georgia, Bugwood.org: page 125 (middle right)

Terri Hughes-Oelrich: page 18

Corina Kanwischer: page 85 (top left)

Julie Michelle/Femme Fotographie: page 92

Rico Montenegro, Chief Certified Arborist, FTPF: pages 42 and 111 (bottom)

Robert L. Morris, University of Nevada Cooperative Extension: pages 135 (right); 137 (right); and 142 (right)

Courtesy of Natural Resources Conservation Service, USDA: page 28

Scot C. Nelson, University of Hawaii at Manoa: page 138

Jay W. Pscheidt: page 122 (bottom)

Connie Pugh, Farm Sanctuary: page 169 (top)

Yuan-Min Shen, Taichung District Agricultural Research and Extension Station, Bugwood.org: page 132 (top)

Jeff Skeirik: pages 93; 149 (top); and 149 (bottom left)

Tim Tigner, Virginia Department of Forestry, Bugwood.org: page 139

University of Georgia Plant Pathology Archive, Bugwood.org: pages 130 (top); 130 (bottom); 131 (top); 131 (middle); and 131 (bottom)

Utah State University Cooperative Extension: page 124 (bottom left)

Carmen Vidal-Hallett: page 89

David Wolfe: page 53 (noni)

ACKNOWLEDGMENTS

This book was made possible through the vision of David "Avocado" Wolfe.

Heartfelt thanks on behalf of fruit trees everywhere to FTPF's talented staff and dedicated volunteers for their contributions to this handbook: Rico Montenegro (chief certified arborist), Robyn du Pré (director of outreach & development), Katherine Drotos (educator), Jill Ettinger (editor), and Juliana Garske (lead photographer & researcher); and to all those who helped in ways not previously mentioned: Tal Ronnen, Lia Ronnen, Diana Stobo, Nancy Dionne, Joseph La Forest, Rochelle Bourgault, Tiffany Hill, and Quarry Books.

Extreme gratitude to FTPF's friends, whose support allows us to plant so many fruit trees for communities and create materials such as this handbook: Jason Aberbach, Steve Adler, Ayça Akın, Cenay Akın, Mete Akın, Su-Mia Fazilet Akın, the Altay family, Marc Anderson, Scott Anderson, Vanessa Barg, Silvia Barretto, Paul Bartlett, Sarah Bartlett, Angela Bassett, Ed Begley, Jr., Daniel Bergan, Biddle's Nursery, Rick Blair, Jeffrey Botticelli, Stephanie Boyles, Gabrielle Brick, James Brown, Sandra Brzozowski, Taylor Call, Karen Cartwright, CleanStar Development, Common Vision, Brendan Daley, Jen Day, Heather Delgado, Neil DiPaola, Lisa Drew, Dreyer's Fruit Bars, The Drip Store, Lauren Ehlert, the Ettinger family, Nathan Feura, Christa Fink, Fortina Chocolate, Lisa Franzetta, Bruce Friedrich, FruitaBü, Michelle Fuller, Severine Fumoux, the Garske family, Camille Rose Giglio, Gnosis Chocolate, Bobby Gonzalez, Kevin Haber, Scott Handleman, Emily Hemingway, Antone Honanie, Hopi Tutskwa Permaculture, Marisa Hormel, Bryce Dallas Howard, Ariana Huemer, Lilian Hill, Humane Society of the United States, Mark Hull, Institute for Integrative Nutrition, Ray Ippolito, Andre de Jesus, Kelly Johnson, Joseph Karanja, the Karasapan family, Kashi, Erin Kavanagh, Lisa Lange, Samantha Leffler, The Longevity Now Conference, Barry Maketansky, Roland Manakaje, Jacobo Marcus, Evan Marks, McGregor Fence Company, Janet McKee, Fernando Medina, Craig Anthony Miller, Val Mizuhara, Canan Mutlu, Ingrid Newkirk, Amber Nicola, Rich Nicola, North Atlantic Books, Jenna Norwood, Jamie Ogden, Orange County Nursery, Tania Pappas, Nyree Parisi, Ashok Pawar, Matt Penzer, People for the Ethical Treatment of Animals, Rupa Raghunath das, Jackie Ralya, Zoe Rappoport, Tracy Reiman, Gaylord Robb, Emily Roberts, Joshua Rosenthal, Sacred Chocolate, Sagun Saxena, Seeds Green Printing and Design, Jeff Shaw, Maria Shriver, Stretch Island Fruit Company, Shawna Stursa, Mary Beth Sweetland, the Tancheff family, Jason Tracy, Damian Valdez, Shashank Verma, Carmen & Emilia Vidal-Hallett, Mitch Wallis, Jean Watson, Aura Weinstein, Robyn Wesley, Anna West, Eugene Weymouth, Robert White Mountain, Peter Wood, Laura Yanne, and so many more!

ABOUT THE AUTHORS

This journey started out for **Cem Akın** as a young boy in his grandmother's cherry tree in Turkey, spending countless summer afternoons sitting atop the canopy, marveling at the notion of seemingly unlimited fruits and natural beauty. That serenity came crashing to a halt one memorable day, quite literally. Yet, despite a painful fall from the third scaffold branch, the seeds had been planted for a deep appreciation of fruit trees. Today, as executive director of the Fruit Tree Planting Foundation, Cem has created charitable programs and planted thousands of trees on five continents—in jungles, deserts, and in between. With degrees from Carnegie Mellon University, including a master of science in public policy and management, and further studies at Cambridge and Cornell, his career in the nonprofit sector has resulted in precedent-setting policy changes and direct benefits for communities in the fields of environmental and animal protection. Cem is an enthusiastic photographer and filmmaker—having codirected PETA's widely distributed documentary short, *Meet Your Meat*.

The good fortune of growing up in rural Southern California led **Leah Rottke** in pursuit of a career spent outdoors. After finishing college, and working twenty-five years in landscape management and the practice of arboriculture, she shares her wealth of experience with her peers through dozens of published articles. Now, Leah enjoys teaching ornamental horticulture at the community college level. She also volunteers as an arborist and educator for local public gardens and gardening organizations. Leah is an ISA Certified Arborist, a graduate of the consulting academy of the American Society of Consulting Arborists, and a member of the Garden Writers Association. She has volunteered her time and expertise to the Fruit Tree Planting Foundation since 2006, and she flood irrigates all of her fruit trees.